The Narrow Way

By

Walter Novak

A
Biography

Order this book online at www.trafford.com
or email orders@trafford.com

Most Trafford titles are also available at major online book retailers.

Note for Librarians: A cataloguing record for this book is available from Library
and Archives Canada at www.collectionscanada.ca/amicus/index-e.html

Printed in Victoria, BC, Canada.

ISBN: 978-1-4269-1575-8 (sc)

*Our mission is to efficiently provide the world's finest, most comprehensive book publishing
service, enabling every author to experience success. To find out how to publish your
book, your way, and have it available worldwide, visit us online at www.trafford.com*

*The Narrow Way: A biography by Walter Novak, printed and copywritten
2008, Annandale, VA 22003 and Zephyrhills, FL 33541.*

Trafford rev. 09/16/2009

Trafford
PUBLISHING®   www.trafford.com

North America & international
toll-free: 1 888 232 4444 (USA & Canada)
phone: 250 383 6864 ♦ fax: 812 355 4082

Contents

Begins with lone harmonica playing *Streets of Loredo*

Hello this is Walter Novak, Walter *A* Novak. The A stands for my dad's name Anthon. I thought I would narrate a few things from my life. I have eight brothers and two sisters. John is the oldest, Jim, Joe and Steve, then I come along--Walt, then Ted and George and Nelly (or Ann), Mary, then the youngest boy Phillip. So there were eight brothers and two sisters and dad and Mother. So I was in the middle somewhere and I always had someone looking after me or me after the others.

Little Boy in Manatoba Forest

I probably deserved a lot what I got from my big brothers. But we always enjoyed each other and always had something to do; either baseball hide-and-seek or many other games in those days. None of them cost anything, except it gave us lots of enjoyment. Doc-on-a-rock was a good game but it hurt my fingers sometimes when the rock came down on my finger rather then the other rock, but that's how it was. I was born in 1917, April 10 to be exact, in a homesteaders cabin that my dad homesteaded and built back in Canada. Manitoba, Canada-- the area of Winnipeg, and the town we were in was Silver. My dad and the two older brothers were loggers. We had 160 acres of virgin woods, and there were many, many good trees there. We lived there, the best I can figure, about six or seven years. Brother Steve was born there and also myself and Ted was born in Canada. So we kind of got hooked on Canada, all of us. Lots of good stories came from there.

We always begged the older boys to tell us more about their adventures up there in the Northern woods. Well, I have an adventure from the days that I was led around by the hand. I could not have been maybe a year and half old, something like that, our cabin, I don't remember the cabin, but our older brother told me, was about 30 ft long and had a clay tamped floor. It became like cement after awhile, and March hay roof. Mother had a cast iron stove. I don't know where she got it up there but apparently they had them in 1917. I remember visiting our neighbor, and his cabin was not too far from our place and I remember it was dark when we were there and my two older bothers and the two next, Steve and Joe. John and Jim were older but they were half brothers. Dad had been married before.

I remember around this cabin were stumps and all around the yard were stumps there were trees apparently cut in winter time above the snow line and now it was summer and the stumps protruded all over the place. They were poplar mainly and poplar is soft wood. It has a lot of phosphate in the roots and the roots will give off light in the night. Like the eyes of a wolf which apparently were plenty of then around there. And this night, Steve and I and Joe were out on the porch of the cabin and we saw these lights around and so we would take hold of hands and see how far we dared to walk out before our fear world get to us and we would run back to the safety of the house. Like I said, the wolf's eyes were the same color as the phosphate. We couldn't tell which was which. That was the game played, to see how far we could walk out before the fear of the wolf got too us. So again I was always lead by the hand.

We had an epidemic of cattle disease after the war. There was a lot of cholera going around, and also the flue pandemic. Just about every family lost somebody. These were hard times and this cattle disease would kill the cows and calves. We needed oxen to transport the logs. So the order came to kill all animals. Kill all the cattle. Dad saved a calf. He was hoping that possibly the disease wouldn't attack this little critter but it did and he had to kill it and burn it. And Steve, Joe and I took hold of hands again and we walked out to see the chard bones that were in the corner of the fence where this calf was cremated. And that still remains with me.

Black Bear Who Liked Sandwiches

Another time, when the men were cutting wood, John and Jim were working as grown men along with dad. I remember them in the evening sharpening their axes. They were never sharp enough until they could shave with them. Shave their arm with them. Then they were ready for cutting.

Mother wanted to bring some lunch to them about mid day and she packed everything into a pillow case which was a carry-all in them days. She also put in a jar of coffee; two quarts with cream and sugar already added. And she took my hand and we went into the woods. I could hear the axes whacking against the trees as we got closer. And I saw my older bother Steve. He was sitting in a middle of a dirt road there, playing with chips. Wood chips and they were as big as saucers. I remember that part of Canada

There are a lot of stories as I said. My uncle lived near there too. Bill Tupish. He had a flock of kids and they were named similar to my brothers. There was George, Ted Mary and Steve. This uncle had been plowing with his oxen near a rail road track. And apparently during lunch time, while he sat there eating his bag lunch, he turned these oxen loose to graze. He finished eating and dozed off and the smell of food attracted a black bear. This bear came nosing around there and stuck his nose into the bag that contained his food. Uncle woke up with the tail of this bear right next to his face and he grabbed a hold of it and the bear tried to get at him. And they went around in a circle. A bear's neck is kind of stiff and he can't turn his neck so he had to turn his whole body. They were going round and around and my uncle was hollering for help. As loud as he could and it aroused the oxen and they came to his help. They charged this bear and drove him off. That is one of the stories I remember. We were all out on the porch listening, wondering what the noise was all about coming through the woods. We did not find out till next day that it was a bear by the tail.

There was this person we had gone to visit (when I said walking out as far as we could). He had been under a bear attack. The bear had tried to get into the house in the worst way. The bear tried to scramble through the window. He finally came to the door. The door would open to the inside. They propped the door up with guns to keep the bear from breaking down the door. And we always thought it was odd that they never shot the bears but apparently some of those bears would take a lot of lead and it wasn't safe to agitate them any more then necessary.

Making a Lime Pit

My dad along with Sandusky, his neighbor, I think, they would get together to build these cabins because it would take more then one man. So they would finish one and then go build the neighbors' cabin. His name was Sandusky. Frank, his name was. And he remained a good friend of ours for a long long time. He even came back to the states with us. One of the things dad use to do, well, they all got in on it, was to start a lime pit. The lime apparently was just a short ways under the top soil. And they would scoop off this soil and build a fire over this white limestone. And they kept the fire going day and night for a certain number of days. It would then break down. The heat would break it down then they would pour water on it and it would form a type of well and anyone who wanted to get lime for painting would get it from here. They used the lime for white washing, sterilizing, beautifying the building, cabins and tools. If tools were whitewashed in the fall, they wouldn't rust up during the winter. So they used this lime pit, all the neighbors did once it was broken down.

Was it a Dog or a Wolf?

In order to break it down they had to make arrangements to take turn to man the fire day and night. Well, this night that dad was manning this fire he fell asleep and when he opened his eyes he was encircled by a bunch of wolves. They were all sitting down. They were curious as to what was going on. He didn't like their company. He took some wood whorl it over his head and they would back off a ways. But I don't think they went very far.

Another thing, we had a dog by the name of Katie over there in Canada, and my brother Steve, next oldest brother to me, he was telling me how mother, dad, Joe and John and Jim were haying and dad would cut the hay. It was marsh hay rather harsh stuff. But the cattle could eat it during winter time especially oxen. But in order to get it out of the swamp, it had to be carried out on your back so the whole family would go and Steve was sitting on a blanket in the corner of the marsh and his dog was with him. The folks would roll up some of this hay into a rope and put it around the small stacks they had that were drying and carry it out where they could load it on the wagon, actually on a sleigh. They didn't have wagons there, at least we didn't.

4

And while my brother Steve was sitting there, he says a wolf came. He thought it was another dog so he called to him. He wanted to pet him. Of course Katie, she recognized that this was a menace and she drove him off. But while she was driving one wolf another one would come up and start nosing around with Steve. Finally the commotion got the attention of the rest of the family. They put an end to it all and drove them out and took Steve out of there. So that was a close one for Steve. The wolves would have walked off with him.

The next thing in my life that I recall was the next town, named Silver. There were several trains and the cars were being shifted around. We were in a type of a station; I don't know if it was another railroad car or a station, I believe it was a station. And my brother Ted was old enough now and he and I were standing there by the window looking at these trains. And they had a strange chimney. It would start up then out and in and then up again. Later they told us they were wood burning engines and the stacks were arranged in that manner to keep the sparks from flying out and setting the place afire. I remember that and at the same time my brother Steve, he saw his first black person. There was a black family there; they had a little girl about his age. He took a hold of her hand and wanted us to see her. They came running across where mother and dad were sitting and they were just having a lot of fun running back and forth. Finally the mother of the girl gave Steve a big red apple. He brought it over and mother cut it up for all of us. I remember that and another thing, we were in a hotel. We were on our way to Michigan. I don't know what exactly which town we were in, but it was evening and my brothers and I were on a balcony looking over the town. There was smoke everywhere, a kind of blue smoke. It would be from burning wood. And everyone was burning wood throughout the whole town. And the whole town was blue from the smoke so that's how it was in those days.

Lone harmonica playing *Do Da Day*

Pioneer Farming in the USA

My folks made arrangements to have a little farm in Michigan. It was close to a little town called Tustin, about two miles, maybe less. Good road. Frank Sandusky came along with us. He had a small family, two girls and a boy. They split the house so both families stayed in the same house and farmed the land there. And they done pretty good. They got along real well. The kids didn't get along that well but the adults did. One nice thing was there was a beautiful lake about a mile or mile and a half away from that farm so we had excellent swimming.

Harvesting Ice

The lake was an ideal place for making ice in the winter time. And what I mean by making ice is, before refrigeration of any kind, the storekeepers and butcher shops would have a room, well insulated and stacked with blocks of ice. And that's where they stored meat and stuff. And I remember one of the ice houses there, I'll tell you about it. We would help make ice. Cut it in squares and they had a horse to pull the wagon or slay rather. They would have the team of horses right there on the lake. And this ice would be quite heavy, maybe 14 or 15 inches thick. It would be cut into maybe, 24X24 inches each piece. Then an ice house would be built on the shore of this lake; made out of logs, no windows. On one side there were a series of doors leading clean to the roof. This was a three story structure. And inside was over laid with sawdust. Over the floor was about 6 or 8 inches of sawdust. Then these blocks would be laid and covered with more sawdust. And this would be built up clean to the roof and these doors would be laid in. Later the top door would be removed and ice would be used. Well whoever helped make this ice, whoever helped cut this ice, he had the privilege of using it during summer.

We didn't use very much. We didn't even own an ice box. But we did own an ice cream freezer and I remember this particular time, it was summer, and Dad had planned a mystery trip for us. Mother was in on it I guess, as she fixed a freezer of ice and a mixture for ice cream. She would make all kinds of ice cream.

6

Real delicious. Of course it was pure cream and in it would be sometimes wild strawberry or sometimes coffee or sometimes chocolate, if we had it. Different berries would be into it. Well, we didn't know where dad was taking us. At first, we thought we would go to the lake, but no, he turned the horses around and headed toward the back end of the farm. And we were all in this wagon, speculating, of course, we had the ice cream freezer and the lunches already.

Then Dad stopped in a beautiful grove and it was cherries, all over the place. He un-harnessed the horses and let them graze and my older brother Joe and mother were making the ice cream it took a lot of cranking and getting things ready for lunch. The rest of us scattered about to pick berries. It was such a nice day, I can just visualize it: sun shining, berries, and the grinding of the ice cream freezer, anticipating eating it. We had just a marvelous day, a break from work, every day work. Well, I was just a little guy. I know how big I was at that time but not how old I was. I couldn't be very old because Ted was next youngest to me and my little brother George was not born yet. He was born on the place. So and of course mother was working with dad, Jim and John in the fields. Joe who was the oldest boy in the house then would watch the children. I recall once that for lunch, Joe had a pie. We were suppose to have it and he carved it up and laid a slab of it on the table for me to eat. And my mouth just fitted to the edge of the table. And he says, "you don't need no spoon or fork, all you need to do is just keep shoving the pie up and chumming away at it." So I wasn't that big so I had a hard time getting over that age, but I made it pretty good.

Dad used to buy sugar in 100 pound bags. White bags and he would set it on a chair in the corner of the house until it could be put away. I remember sneaking behind that chair and taking a corner of the bag in my mouth and sucking the sugar and that was my pacifier until finally they caught me at it and of course that was the end of that.

So we had a kind of a cellar, it had two sets of stairs one going to the neighbors and one to our kitchen. Dad had bought several crates of apples, beautiful apples. We had them down in the basement and I took a box… oatmeal box. I would put apples in them and carry them up the other stairs and I would give them to Sandusky and their family and of course they world pat me on the head and say, "go get us some more, get us some more." And then somebody caught me doing it and my atta-boys went out the window right a way.

Anther time I was playing next to the road there. It was a nice place to play at. There were trees along the road, then there was a gate. I was outside the gate on the road side. There was a big rock there and I would pick up dandelions and put them on the rock and smash them with another stone. And I called it my factory, I was play'en. And I would pick up another bunch of dandelion blossoms and smash them with the stone. Well this day Ted came along and he kept putting his finger on this rock between my blows. Well it didn't turn out just exactly right and I hit his finger with the rock. Well, he went home and didn't really explain to the folks what happened. Apparently they got the message that I hit him with a rock which was a no-no. So here comes dad to give me my grubb'en. Well, I started running away, around the house and I imagine I had my siren on, full blast. But I was runn'en and every time I looked over my shoulder, Dad was just ready to grab me, and I'd put on more speed and more noise and I ran around the corner and he had pressed himself against the wall and he was waiting for me. And I was shocked! I thought he was right behind me and there he was standing right in front of me. I really didn't have a chance. Well, he swatted me once on the pants and took off. I guess he got his jollies out of it but it wasn't so jolly for me.

King David's Sling Shot

There was another incident and John and Jim were sawing wood and it was in our yard and they had a saw horse and a box saw and they were cutt'en it up, stove size. And Jim, he, had a King David sling shot it was a couple of thongs hooked to leather. One of these thongs were hooked to his wrist and the other go around his finger and he could whorl this around his head and let go with one finger and this stone would go a hurling a great distance. And he bet his brother John, that he could hurl this stone clean over the house. So then they made this bet and he found a stone he liked and he sent it a fly'en. And it didn't quite make it but it did make it to the bay window of the house. Dad was sitting there reading his paper all the time. So here he comes. (Dad had had an accident back in the Northern woods. He cut his toe off with that sharp ax of his and it healed but it didn't heal correctly so he had to wear Artics, rubber winter boots, (winter and summer.) And of course they weren't buckled up and he would be walking like a giant with those big feet. Here he comes. So he grabbed John and began to pound him. I said, "whoo, wait a minute. It wasn't John. It was Jim." So he let go of John and took hold of Jim and started pounding him. Well I began to feel sorry for Jim so I said, "No. No. It was John." Then he started reaching for me. All I could do was start running between his legs and I got away that time as fast as I could go.

Well, John and Jim, in desperation, almost anything would bring a clog across the head or a kick in the pants. This time they were carving and they used the kitchen knife and the kitchen knife broke. So they knew they were going to get it. And Dad had a belt, a rather nice one with a silver buckle and he'd use it on them once in a while. He'd fold it up and use it. So they felt they were going to get it with the belt and they about had enough of it so they took the belt and cut it into little pieces. Oh, about 6 inches long. It barely hung together. When dad found out that they had broken the knife he reached for the belt and it fell apart in his hands. He stood there baffled. He couldn't quite believe it. And when I saw him standing there, to my surprise I walked over there and I asked him if I could have the buckle and he handed it to me. So that was something.

The house wasn't quite finished. It was a huge thing. And some of the back rooms were used for a bed room but it didn't have a ceiling. And the 3 of us, Joe, Steve and I, this night, we were laying in the bed and got the giggles about something. You know how it is when you get the giggles, you can't stop. And dad and mom and I guess there was someone else there, they were trying to have a conversation but the giggling…they warned us several times to stop it. But it was no use. So I hear the big boots coming again. So I scooted under the bed and of course the 2 kids Joe and Steve got as far from the edge of the bed as they could and he had to reach to get at them. I was holding them up because the springs were almost reaching the floor. And I was in between the springs and the floor. He couldn't find me that time. But sometimes he'd poke me with a broom when I was under the bed. And that was one of my hiding places.

Mysterious Watch

There was a strange ticking noise in the house. It sounded like a well made watch: very neat ticking in this house. My brother John was always searching for this watch. He wanted to find it. Couple years later when we bought another farm, several miles away, and we moved, that watch went along with us. It kept ticking in our new house. I remember one time dad said, "It must be an echo from the big clock. I'm going to stop the big clock and see if the noise goes away." And he held the big clock from operating but the other ticking didn't go away. It sounded like it was up in the ceiling. One morning I was in bed alone. Everyone had gone someplace, and I heard that thing. I stood up so I could be closer to the ceiling. It seemed like it was off in a corner but as I stood up and got my head closer to the ceiling the thing just went whirring and it came right over the top of my head and started ticking. Man! I took off out of there.

Besides that sugar sack that I used as a pacifier, I'd also eat clay. The house had been chinked with clay and I'd bread off a hunk in the back of the house and it seemed to satisfy me. There was something in it that my body really needed. Of course I'd get caught, get beat up and they'd wash my mouth out and then I'd go to the lime barrel and do the same thing with lime. Its strange how a person would seek something that is lacking.

Little Brother George

Ted and I were getting along pretty good but we needed another brother because we wanted to play three handed poker and other games. And then George was born so we kind of took over. I guess we got him to walking about 8 or nine months. He was awfully little. I remember our Mother made our overalls. She sewed most of our clothes. She'd get the material from Sears Roebuck. Make shirts and overalls. She ran out of material for George so she made him a pair with only one suspender, instead of two. And he liked that very well because he could undress faster then any of us. Or put on his cloths faster then any of us. He had only one suspender. He was with us all the time. Ted and I would haul him around. We got him to talking. We could understand what he was saying but no one else could. So we would have to interpret for him when he asked for something. Like pupa pupa meant cup of coffee. But no nobody else knew what he was saying, just Ted and I. Hind-dea meant he wanted some milk. So we had to interpret for him.

Little People's Entertainment

Joe and Steve, they always wanted to take off somewheres and they would have trees like mulberry trees or choke cherry trees which was real good when they were ripe. They would sneak off and come back with this good stuff but I never knew where they were getting it. They would never take me. This one time I wanted to go with them but in order to get rid of me they'd climb upon the chicken coop roof. This was a flat roof. They'd lay there and admire the clouds and the sky and say, "Oh, how beautiful it looks from here because we are so much closer to these clouds. They look so much better then from the ground." I said," take me up there. Take me up there." So they'd oblige and pull me up there on the roof and jump off and run. I couldn't get off that darn thing. I'd get stuck up there. When I finally drop down it would hurt my belly and they would be gone by then.

Tape One, Side B

Ted George and I would play cards. Harmonica playing.

We would cut up fake dollar bills out of paper. We would sit on the floor, the three of us. We would play poker. Dad walked in one time. He stood looking it over and he got interested in it. He said, "Get me some money." So we gave him a wad of it and he would play it. And he would be betting all the time. I would look at his face to see if I could recognize if he was bluffing or not. But he was really poker face. You couldn't read his mind. I think most of the time he was bluffing but he played with us till he took all our money. I am surprised on how he was interested in it. Another time, they always had stove wood and some of it would be round; about two inch round cherry. We would cut off a piece four inches long and cut a hole in it. And we'd make croquet hammers for ourselves. And then we would play croquet, the three of us. Then, the older folks came along and John, Jim and dad. They couldn't resist it. They took our hammers away from us and put on a little too much English and of course broke our handles. It is amazing how kids can fix up something for themselves, if there is anything available.

Kidnappers

There was one incident that happened; I can't figure it out myself. There was a dip along side of the road. I think they took dirt out of there to fill in somewhere. And it was overgrown with beautiful grass. Just as green, blue green, and Joe and I and Steve, we'd go play in this hole next to the road. And it was maybe two blocks from home. Joe, Steve and I were there and a carriage went by pulled by one black horse. It had curtains in it and two men were in it. And it spooked Joe. He was telling us about kidnappers: They would pick up kids and break their arms to get sympathy and then send them out on the street to collect money for them. I don't know where he got this story from but a short time later this carriage was coming back and Joe broke into a run for home and he did not run down the road but ran next to the fence. Over a bank and he was gone. And Steve was next running away, the same way and he got to the top of this knoll and stopped to look back for me. Well my legs were short and I couldn't run very fast. This carriage stopped and this guy jumped out and he grabbed me by the head and put his hand over my mouth. He was dragging me to this carriage. Well, then I heard this guy inside this carriage, he gave a command. The fellow dragging me wanted to argue with him. The command came more fiacre and he let me go. I think they did that because Steve was taking it all in from the top of this hill. He could see what was going on so they released me. We never did find out who they were or what happened.

Mounting a Horse

I use to like horses. I still do. And as a little chap I would walk out into the pasture hoping I could catch the horses lying down. If I could catch them laying down then I could climb up on their back. The horses tolerated me. They would get up and come back to the house for water. They would come and get their drink and give me a ride. Sometimes I would come charge'n. My brother Joe would look at me and say, "How did you get up on this horse?" Boy! When I had to get down again I would hold on to the main and reach down as far as I could and still I had to drop down to the ground. It always hurt my belly but it was fun riding those animals. Later on when I got older I use to sneak one of the horses out of the barn. It was a beautiful little mare. I think she enjoyed this about as much as I did. I did her a favor one time. She was paw'en at a woven wire fence in the pasture near the railroad track. I think she tried to get where the grass was greener. She was paw'en at this fence and the wire got caught between her hoof and horseshoe. And she was stranded there. I don't know what I was do'en there but I was passing by and seen her there. And I removed the wire so she could get away. Later I would ride her sometimes, sneak her out of the barn and ride her over to the neighbors to make a date with one of the girls there. I looked pretty good there on the little horse. But if my dad would have caught me he would have skinned me alive.

Cows Coming Home for Milking

Dad had bought another farm. It was on the north end of Tustin about two miles on the right side. It was 80 aches. It had 2 ponds on it. We moved in there. It also had a rail road track going through the center of it; 40 ache's on one side and 40 aches on the other side of the track. It was a nuisance because of the gates we had to open. The railroad was fenced in and we had to open two gates to get across to the other side which we were constantly doing. But another thing, it was nice in the winter time because when it snowed the track was always plowed. Not like the road. We could always walk to town on the track about two miles. That made it good too. It was interesting. There were these two trains would go by. One wound go by at 12 o'clock and one would go by at 1:30. So we would time ourselves as to when to stop the field work to go home for lunch. One train would go by then at 1:30 when the horses had time to eat and we had our lunch, we would go back to work. We timed ourselves by the trains.

We were kids yet. I wasn't going to school yet and in the evening the cows would come home to be milked. Their utters would be heavy and full of milk. And they were uncomfortable and they wanted to be milked. They would come to the barn, actually to the barn yard and stand around. The mosquitoes were very prevalent. Pestilence! And so we would start a smoke fire while mother and dad and older boys Joe and Steve would be milking, and the cows would be standing untied. The milkers would just go from one cow to another and the younger kids, myself, George and Ted would pick up dried cow dung and put it on the fire to cause this smoke. And the cattle would stand in this smoke and it would drive the mosquitoes away to some extent. To me it was always a nice time of day. It was cool in the evening and the family would be together. We were all busy. The older people would be milking, us youngsters would be keeping the fires going--such a pleasant chore.

Individual Attention

Harmonica: **Barney Goggle, with the** *Googly Googly Eyes.*

When I was a little kid, my dad, he was close to nature, I guess, he would like to lie down in a shady spot and take a little snooze now and then. And I would sneak upon him and lay down on his back. And I would sleep and then when he would wake up, he would just grab me by the legs and carry me home on his back. So that was being a little close with our dad then. Another thing he use to do, he would go to town about once a week with the horses and he would deliver milk and eggs or whatever we had for sale and pick up groceries. He would take one of my brothers with him and eventually it would be my turn and he would give us a close relationship in that manner. And when we'd get to town, why, he'd usually slip us a nickel for candy. And we could choose whatever type of candy we wanted. This grocery store was very unique because it contained everything anyone needed in them days. And this Anderson, the owner, would take in cream and eggs and any cattle we wanted to sell like pigs and chickens and cows. He had his own slaughter house. He had some acreage somewhat away from town and that's where he would take them and slaughter them and cut the meat up. The duffle would go to the pigs. He'd have pigs underneath the slaughter house and they would clean it up. So he was make'n money every way he could. He had a daughter. Her name was Iris; the one girl. And she was exceptionally generous with us kids. When ever she would be behind the candy counter, no mater how little money you had, she would always fill the bag up full of candy. Once in a while her mother would catch her at it and would dump it back out and give us the proper amount. But she was always sneak'en candy to us whenever she could from her store.

Muck-Garden

The original farm that we were farming with our neighbor there, was called, "Bextrum's Place". These farms, no matter who owned them or for how long, were usually called by the original homesteaders. Like Hoosder's Place. The place we were on now was called "Anderson Farm". Like I said, about 80 archer farm. We did pretty good on that farm. There was a kind of a marshy area and dad farmed it. It was muck next to the rail road track. Dad ditched it and drained it and planted it into garden stuff. I never saw anything grow like that. And he was quite a farmer and gardener. in the winter time, he would go to in Harvy, Illinois and work in the foundry or operate railroad engines in the railroad yards. In the summer time he'd have to get out into the farm where there was soil and he could see things grow. So he knew muck farming. He said he could grow more on an acre of muck then on 20 acres of regular ground, which is true. And he supplied vegetables for everyone. All the neighbors would come by. Green lettuce! Oh! That was so delicious. Onions, radishes, everything you could think of would grow abundantly there.

But within a year, a train caught this muck on fire. The sparks ignited it. It was dry on the top. It caught on fire and burned clear down to the very bottom in spite of everything the railroad could do. They would bring cars full of water, hoses and they would try to put this fire out that was under ground. It would burn persistently, straight down through the good soil. He got some compensation for it, not very much. Eventually it started growing back into brush and dad hated to see it grow back into brush so he sent Ted and George and me out there to pull out the brush. We worked on it all day and could not make any headway. And of course, I was in charge then. I was the oldest. Somehow I got the idea of dividing and conquering. So I divided this area into three pieces; one for George, one for Ted and one for myself. The object was, whoever finished his piece first could go home. And you know it didn't take us long to finish it. When we divided it and we really went at it hard and learned a little lesson there: on your own property you work a lot harder then you would in community.

Flower Pot Potato Farm

We raised mainly potatoes on our acreage. They would be in rows and cross cultivated and hoed and hilled up so each looked like a flower pot and the field was really a garden. Looked like a garden Dad wouldn't stand a weed in his field. Of course he had plenty of boys and he had a hoe for each one of us. So we kept it really top shape got all the crop the land could possible produce.

We enjoyed our ponds. Ideal for swimming in the summer time and for catching frogs and turtles but this was winter time and Steve, Joe and I went out to see if the ice was thick enough for skating and it was kind of rubbery. We'd get on it, and again we were holding hands because it was little bit treacherous if it would break down. And we would skate across and it would billow in front of us. And we decided it was rubbery ice and held up in good shape. So we started playing pom-pom pull-a-way. The object was to catch a person then you would have to hit him three times on the back before he would come over on your side and we were play'en away and Steve and I caught Joe. But he wouldn't allow us to hit him on his back. He laid down on the ice on his back and we tried to roll him over then Steve was on top of him and I was on top of Steve. Then the inevitable happened! The ice broke down. And of course I was able to climb out first because I climbed up on Steve's shoulder. I heaved myself up on sound ice. Steve followed me but poor Joe had to lay there on his back in the mud until we all cleared off before he could finally make it. We all got home like wet rats. Had to strip and dry our cloths out around the fire. But we had fun!!

George, Ted and I had a garden. It was near the house. And together we paced off a plot and we put some fence posts in around the thing and got some rusty barbed wire that we picked up somewheres. And we fenced it in real good so the cattle couldn't get in there and disturb our crop. We would put in rutabagas, onions and potatoes but first we would work the ground. We had to take off all the top sod because we had no way of working it or anything. So we had a couple piles of this sod stacked up there in the corner. And then we would go to the chicken coop and clean it. We took all the manure out of it. Mother never had such a clean chicken coop as when we had a garden. That was not enough; we'd go to the swamp there and get turf; decayed matter there from the swamp and haul it and spread it over the garden and work it in. So we had pretty good soil there when we planted. We were pretty proud of it. We worked it every day, when we had time. Dad would insist on us keeping the crab grass and weeds out of there too. It had to be up to his standard otherwise he wouldn't be too proud. We were always trying to please him, that atta-boy, the pat on the back, which was so dear to us but came so seldom.

Lessons Learned Behind Barbed Wire

But this time the three of us would combine forces and we would sometimes pick on our older brother Steve who was not much older then myself. Maybe a little over a year but somehow he had the mentality of an adult. And he would also have the capacity to work and keep up with grown men. No matter how hard I tried, I never could catch up to him. He always was somewhat ahead of me. So sometimes we would get into scraps and I would call on my two younger brothers and we could clean up on Steve. He didn't have a chance against the three of us but sometimes he would catch us alone and would pound us pretty good.

So dad would be sitting in his bay window smoking and meditating and he could see and understand everything that was going on his domain. He caught on to what was going on so he called Jim and Joe and Steve together onetime and he said, "You guys better straighten those youngsters out. They're getting a little cocky." Well we somehow recognized a menace when we seen it. They got together and started marching toward us. We crawled into our garden, under the fence. There were so many wires there that they couldn't get through to us. Especially when we had dirt clods and we just peppered them, to keep them out. We were desperate kids there but they were desperate too. The more we would pound them, the more angry they became and finally they broke through that wire. We couldn't get out. We forgot to make a passage on the other side. They had a hold there and we couldn't run away. We were fenced in once they got in. Each older brother took one of us kids and did we ever get it. My brother Joe was my tormentor there. I never forgot the beating I got there. It straightened us out. There was no more of that!

Outsmarted by a Bird

I was wandering around the pound. And I saw this bird with a broken wing and awaaa, he was so pitiful. He'd lay on his side and stretch out his broken wing. Cried and move over a little bit and cry some more. I tried to catch him and bring him home and have mother take care of him but no matter how hard I tried, I couldn't quite make it. So I figured I better tell dad about it. Dad would take care of animals like that. And I told him at supper time about the bird out there. He kind of laughed, "That bird is fooling you. It's a Snipe. And he's leading you away from his nest." Of course I didn't believe him so I went up there again. And sure enough, that bird was there. So I kept chasing him and this time I put on a little more speed and sure enough he kept backing up, backing up until he got me far enough away from his nest and up he went into the air. There was nothing wrong with him at all. Strange!

Garbage Dump Library

I don't know when I learned to read. Mother used to order elementary books from Wisconsin. That's where we got our newspaper from, and she would teach us how to read polish. There were pictures in it. It was made of cloth material instead of paper. And so we learned polish even before we tackled English. But somewhere along the way, I learned to read. Only thing was, there was nothing for children to read. Only Polish newspaper, that's all and that wasn't too interesting for us. It usually had a serial going like "Wolf" or different animal stories and Mother would read to us. But there wasn't anything for children so what I did was wander through the woods up by our neighbors place, there way a dump there. The person who owned it was called Oddleson and he had a farm there, a very hilly farm that he farmed and so I would go down to the dump and read the old newspapers that had Uncle Wiggly and stories like that in it which I could read. That was the only place I could find anything to read. And also I liked to walk the roads. All these roads were through swamps. The way they would make a road was they would lay logs parallel and then they would dig a ditch on either side and throw the dirt on these logs. And that would be firm enough to drive horses and wagons and eventually cars even, with additional gravel. And I would walk these roads. It was almost like through tunnels I was looking for quail. These birds would come out on the road, the mother quail and her little ones. And her little ones were yellow color chicks. And they had one feather coming from the tops of their heads. I always wanted to catch these things but no matter how fast I would run, or how hard I would try to sneak up on them, they'd just get off the road into the swamp and just disappear. Every one of them would be gone. You'd think I could catch one little one. But no. They'd all disappear.

I was tell'en my cousin that one time, George, he was older then me. And he said that they run and grab a leaf and turn over on their backs and hold this leaf over their body but I didn't know if I could believe him or not. This time I was walking down this road going home from the woods where Oddlson lived and he came down with his Model-T Ford, he saw me walking;

of course I wasn't wearing shoes. None of us wore shoes in the summertime because we preferred it that way. Besides we didn't have very good shoes anyway. And no shirt. We didn't need no shirt. I don't know if we ever had any underclothes or not. Probably not. At least not the youngsters.

And I was walking along hoping I could catch one of these quails and Oddlson came by and asked me if I wanted to ride and I said, "No, I prefer to walk." And he called me a "hero". I don't know where he got that from. But later when I got a little older and the work was done in the fall, I would go down to his place and help him dig potatoes. I would pick them up and help him haul it in. And he gave me a few nickels. He didn't have any money either, it was hard times. So I'd save it up and then send to Sears Roebuck and buy me a shirt and a belt. I wanted a wide belt all the time. I could never get enough money but this time I did. We called them cowboy belts and of course every one of us needed one. When one got one the others had to get one too.

One Penny with Two Tails

My brother Steve came along, I don't know where he got his money from but he would come with a penny or two and he'd want to flip with me. And he'd always take what ever pennies I had. He'd always win. But this time I took one cent and I filed it down about half way and another one half way and I took it down to town to my older brother who knew how to solder and I asked him to solder the two pennies together so they would be both tails. And he did such a nice job that you couldn't tell. So I had one penny with two tails. So I went back and flipped with Brother Steve and about the third penny he got suspicious. He grabbed it, looked at it, and it had tails on both sides and he stuck it in his pocket and I never saw my penny again.

Over on the farm, original place, before we moved, over there on Anderson farm, there was a little girl born into our family. First little girl, of course everyone was elated. I remember them naming her but I never remember any of the kids being born. Somehow they would spirit the rest of us away and we wouldn't know during the event that it was happening until we got a little brother or sister and they would present the new baby to us. My dad would always start making a new cradle, a rocker, a potty chair and it was one of those things that never lasted from one child to the other. He always made a new one for each kid. We should have caught on when he was working on those cradles. Always had a cradle and one of us would have to rock the baby when it was crying and it seemed like it was crying all the time. Oh, we hated that job. Sometimes I'd tie a string to the cradle so I could walk around and still rock it without needing to hover over it. Dad, he wanted to make something for his little girl so he made her a pair of booties. He made them out of his hat. He cut up his felt hat! Inside of this hat was red so she had a pair of little red booties that he made for her. And that was on Bextrom's Place. Now we were living on our own 80 aches.

School at Last!

Well, as we got older, two kids going to school, Joe and Steve, and they'd tell us all the wonders of what was going on in school. I couldn't wait to go and gradually, gradually, I talked mom into letting me go. Well, I was well prepared because Mother spoke Ukrainian and dad spoke Polish and we mostly spoke those two languages and she made sure I knew how to write and read in Polish. In Polish you don't need to learn to spell, you just sound out the words. So I was a really confused kid. I knew how to write my name but it was in Polish, Wadislowe Nowak. It rattled half way across the board. The teacher look'en at it asked, "What is that?" My bother said, "That's his name in Polish.." And she said, "Well, I'm going to give you a new name." So she called me "Walter." I liked that. It's much shorter and easier to spell then Wadislowe. So it was *School days, school days, good old golden rule days. Reading and writing and arithmetic.* That's about it. Whatever else you learned behind the school house also counted. It was alright. It was atypical one room school with a bench in front of teacher's desk and that where the recitation would take place. And the classes were from one to eight. And after eight years they would be ready for high school class. They would sit in front of the rest of the children and recite their lessons that they had learned, or should have learned. Spelling was my worst subject. But I still believe it was because of the Polish way of spelling. I never did get over that. I still can't spell. Well, the school was the, like I said, a school bell on top and one big heater in back that heated the whole thing. It had an outside vent running to the outside. My brother Ted use to like to crawl under the vent and he would sing cowboy songs and they would amplify through the heater. You could hear him through out the whole school. The teacher would really love that. She would sit there by the heater listening to Ted's cowboy song.

The floor would be freshly waxed and all the seats would be washed clean and a clean school. I'm not sure they waxed it. They may have oiled the floor. And of course we were all barefooted and we would come in there and the floor would feel cool. So nice. I liked that part the best.

Nothing too difficult in school except maybe diagramming. I never could catch on to that and they really didn't insist on me learning it. Just do the best I could on other subjects, alright. And of course reading was my best subject and writing. I could write well until the push and pull system came out, The Palmer Method. They'd start teaching how to use your whole arm to write with instead of writing with my wrist. We had a woman teacher up to the last year I was in school there, then we had a very nice man teacher and he would teach us athletics. He'd put up jumps outside and things like that. Things we never had before. And it was typical. Good days, bad days. Winter time, sliding, tobogganing, building forts, snowballing each other.

Christmas time was really exciting time for me. For all of us I guess. We would slowly cease studying and practice our parts. The neighbor would bring in planks and sawhorses and put up a stage. And then we would have our play for the evening. For all our parents would come and enjoy the evening. And of course we needed a Christmas tree. So the eighth graders and seventh graders would go to find one. And this time Brother Joe came over with Harold his buddy and they said, "We have a tree but we need the rest of the boys to help bring it in." which we really looked forward to. So they got us all out of the school too. We wandered around in the woods, goof'en around until almost 4 o'clock when we had to go home and then we chopped down the first tree we come to. We come dragg'en that thing in… way too big for the school. The teacher had to admire it whether it was good or not. We knew it was too big. So we had to cut the top off and part of the bottom off and put the stub in there and decorate it. We decorated the windows and then we would have our play. We would always have the Santa Clouse come. And we'd choose up names and get something, a pencil or a tablet for whoever we were going to buy a present for. And we'd always receive a bag of candy and peanuts: hard candy and peanuts and a present from some other boy. Usually checkers. One would get the checkers and the other one would receive the board.

Tape 2, Side A

School days were a bit difficult for us youngsters. One of the things was that we didn't get any help from our parents with our homework. Being of Ukrainian and Polish descent, they couldn't help us. And as far as the older brothers, you know how that is. They have their own things to do. And the kid is left on his own to hunk along the best he kin. And when the teacher has a room full of kids, they can't give you personal attention either. But in spite of all that I hunked through grade school some how. And I was very glad, hoping I could go to high school which was in town, Tustin and I understood they had a library there. In the school that I just completed they had one book, Kazan by Oliver Curwood. It was about the only readable book they had there. I know at one time the teacher was burning books by the dozen in a big furnace because they were so out dated and old they were useless for the school children.

So I looked forward to the going to high school but when I asked my dad about it, he says, "I need you on the farm." So that was that. And Mother had passed away then. She had two other children since Nelly (Ann) was born, she had Mary, our other sister, then a little boy Phillip. Of course he was little. Then she had ruptured appendicitis and she passed away shortly after that. And she was quite a woman.

Mother's Premonition

She used to send us to town to get the mail which was a two mile walk, there and back. It would be four miles, to pick up the mail. The mail wasn't delivered in our area. She would know when there would be a letter there from her family in the old country. She could sense whenever a letter was there and if it was a notice of someone's death in the family, she would know it ahead of time. She would already be crying and she wouldn't know which member would be passed away. So she would send us to town to pick up this letter. Many things she could do. She'd have dreams. Our youngest sister Mary when she was a baby she had a stroke and we didn't know what to do. Mother heated up some water and she bathed her in warm water until she came around. And when I asked her how she knew what to do, she said she had a dream the night before. And another thing, my brother John, the oldest, he use to do a lot of traveling around mostly on freight trains. And he would seldom, if ever, write home. So we didn't know where he was and this time, around supper time, Mother said, "John is coming." She began to prepare extra food and keep the coffee warm. Oh, I'd say, within 15 to 20 minuets he was at the door. And she could tell. She could sense.

She raised ten children, eight of her own. She died early. I'd say about 38 when she passed away. She had born eight children and daddy missed her very much.

Yards of Fish

We had a great family life when we were all together. Fishing trips. Dad use to love to go fishing and there were a couple lakes not too far away. And us boys would get the fish poles ready, and we would dig the bate. We had a car at that time and tie the poles to the side of the car. And take off. I would go along with them if I woke up early enough. If I didn't wake up early enough they wouldn't wake me but slip away very carefully. Sometimes I'd run outside and they'd be leav'en. Just past the gate, they'd wave back at me but wouldn't stop. So I had to get up early and my job would be to pick up the fish and deliver the worm or the bate to the fisherman. John, Jim, Steve, Joe and dad would do the fishing. And they kept me busy. They'd say, "Here's one. Here's one. Come and get it." And I'd have to run over there pick up the fish and string it on a string and keep it in the water and deliver a bate to them. That was fun. When we would get home we would have yards of fish and we would clean um and have one big fish fry.

Mother could really fry with onions with a little salt and pepper on um. They really went down good. It was crowded in the house, so in the summer time we use to sleep in a granary, a building a few yards away from the house. The older boys, Joe Steve and Jim would sleep in the balcony. I made me a bunk lower down. Sometime during the night we would visit the neighbors grape vines and help ourselves to his grapes. We felt we were safe from dad catching us as long as we were away from home. One time I heard a strange noise. It woke me up in this granary. And it was coming closer and closer. Most indescribable noise. It scarred me to death. Howling like a wolf or a coyote or dog and it kept coming closer and closer. It was an ungodly sort of noise. And I was sweating in my bed. Finally it went past the door and kept right on a'goen. I was very glad. Next day, neighbor boy he was asking us if we had heard this animal during the night. And it was him. He rode horse back past this granary on his way to town and thought he would give us a thrill by scarring the pants off us. He succeeded alright!

When Farm Work would Slack Off

Around July when the farm work would slack off, before the harvesting, we would go camping at Traverse City cherry orchard peninsula, in northern Michigan. We would stay there maybe a week and come back home on the weekend. And go back again about three weeks and pick cherries for so much a lug. It usually would be my dad, John, Jim, Joe, Steve and me. And dad would do the cook'en up there. It turned out that he was a very good cook. Surprised us. We would work within a half hour of lunch time and then he would break off and within half hour he would have lunch ready for us. He would then call us.

We would work until about 5 o'clock which in the summer time was a rather long evening. And we would go to Lake Michigan to swim. It was walking distance. So it was very enjoyable for us to take this break and also it would make some extra money. We saved up enough to build a barn after a few years of picking cherries.

The person we were working for was called Ben Gearing. He and his family were very nice people to work for. Next farm was George Harvey and some of our neighbors would be working there. So we would get together in the evening just to have a good time with one another. But the hard times were coming: The depression. Banks were beginning to close and it was difficult to get any money at all for circulation. Very few factories were open any longer. No one could afford to buy anything. But on the farm we could always eat. We had our own meat and milk and cream and so on but the city people had it much harder, I believe.

CCC Days (Civilian Conservation Corp)

Franklin Delano Roosevelt was elected president and he started the CCC: The Civilian Conservation Corps. Which were camps scattered all over United States. And they were operated by the army and also the forestry. If you were in camp you were under the jurisdiction of the army officers. And during the working days out in the woods or out in the fields, road work, or fire prevention towers, all of this was part of the job of the CCC. Mostly tree planting really, but they would do a lot of other things too. And so my brother Steve was the first one to join the CCCs and naturally I followed up so dad would receive $25.00 from each of us, per month. And we would receive $5.00 for our spending money, which was sufficient because everything was furnished. And there were opportunities for advancements and also for various jobs.

And one thing I liked, I thought I liked, was being a night guard. It would relieve me of the monotonous job of chopping, thinning out brush, or planting trees. It gave me a chance to roam the woods during the day. And that's what I become, a night guard. And strange thing was, I wasn't told my duties and at the end of the month there was an inspection and they inspected the power house. And it was all fowled up. There was an engine running there providing electricity. And I wasn't told I was in charge of this machine. It must have been running 2 or 3 days without anyone looking in on it. Anyway they looked in on it and the floor needed sweeping and so on. They said,

"You're not doing your job. We'd better find somebody else." I said, "wait a while, wait a while, I didn't know that this was supposed to be my project too. I thought I was just a guard." They said, "No, you're going to have to take care of this. So we'll give you a chance to clean it up." So I cleaned it up. I shined it up. And it was my pride and joy to keep that machine going. To have it shined up, I enjoyed that part of it. And they never had any trouble with me along that line. I would check the barracks. I'd walk through the barracks and make sure the fires were turned down and everyone was sleeping. It was a good job. Toward morning I would start the fires for the cooks. They had three coal burning cook stoves and I would have to get the fires going and get the coffee waters on and wake the cooks. As soon as they were awake, I was free to go to sleep or do whatever I wanted until night time again. That worked out real good for me. And then later on I was driving the tractor, plowing the furrows for the tree planters. I enjoyed that too.

I was collecting butterflies at that time. There were ample moths and butterflies, beautiful ones through out the Huron forest. And I would have to plow a furrow and space out about eight feet and then come back to plow the other one. And I'd carry a butterfly net along. If I saw a nice moth, I'd stop the tractor, chase it down and catch it. I had a book that I cut a notch out for the butterfly body and then I would spread the wings and the wings would dry real nice. I had a pretty nice collection. I remember this one time I was chasing this moth, I had the tractor shut off and the boss came along driving a model A roadster. He come by, I looked up and there they were, a couple foresters sitt'en in their car watching me chase this butterfly. I was surprised they didn't say anything to me.

In this camp the buildings were very rustic. They were built out of pine. All made of wood. The drive way had two big logs diamond shape formation over the entrance. Very picturesque. For the walls, the tree trunks were split and off set. They were nailed together with tar paper in between which made a nice building. You could smell the pine. The tables and benches were all made out of the same material, green pine boards or plank. So the barrack was typical army barracks, tar paper. They were sufficient. They were warm in the winter. They were heated by oil barrels. A three barrel stove. They supplied plenty of heat. That part was good. We had mess kits. We'd eat out of mess kits, personal mess kits. And they'd have a man designated to heat water for washing them and one barrel of boiling water would be with soap in it and chlorine we would first wash our mess kits in that then they had two clear water tubs for rinsing them We had to take care of our own dishes that way. Well, I got interested in cooking later on so I got in there as a 3rd cook. These two boys who were first and second cooks were excellent and very conscientious.

I never saw such conscientious cooks in my life. They were still young boys but they'd be up every morning, early and they'd do an excellent job of providing good meals. Moreover and above what the minute called for all the time, my job as a third cook was to make sandwiches for the boys that were working out in the woods. And it would consist of… first what I would do was open up a loaf of bread and lay it out on the table like cards across maybe two tables. Then there would be a bucket of melted butter and a brush and I'd dab each piece with the butter. I had sliced up meat. Cold cuts usually, and put two or three cold cuts on it then put two pieces of bread on top of this sandwich which would be the base for the second sandwich. I'd go on to make three sandwiches a piece, for each person. Then we'd pack them with wax paper and put them in thermal cans they had there.

Then there would usually be a stew or baked beans or something like that to go along with the sandwiches and coffee. And I'd have to have this ready and accompany the food to the woods and set these containers out and designate some boys to serve. They'd squat down behind each container and dish it out one on each side as the people would walk by. The boys would usually have a bon fire going and a forked stick for their sandwiches. First of all there would be a trading. Everyone would be trading sandwiches. They'd trade a meat sandwich for dog sandwich. Dog would be ground up meat. They would toast them over this fire before they would eat them. It was pretty nice: the smell of burning pine, good coffee, extra strong. So that was my job to begin with and gradually-gradually I worked into a second cook actually I served as a mess sergeant once in a while. And eventually I went to a side camp which had about

30 men in it. And they were foresters. It was kind of an office. And I cooked for them, alone, I didn't have any relief. I cooked for them all by myself. I could cook well except I couldn't bake cakes. They'd all fall down for me and I would fill the cavity with frosting but it didn't work. They wouldn't accept it. Finally one of the foresters, a young boy, he came up and he would make the cakes. I never saw cakes so beautiful, how they'd come out. It never failed for him. And he'd make two of them and frost them with chocolate or vanilla frosting. Just A-1 cakes. What I would do to learn something like that.

Heavy, The Mind Reader

So time was going by and money started circulating and the boys began to save up to buy a car or their parents would buy them a car and then they would start drifting away. But one person that I met there I'll tell you about him. His name was Heavy. I met him when I first went into the CCC and he had been working in the woods. He had come in with his jacket on yet and the boys had told me that he was a mind reader. And I was curious so I was waiting for him to come in from work and I asked him if he would show me a trick. And he would deal out three cards and ask me to think of one and he would tell me which one I was thinking. And sometimes I tried to fool him and keep my mind blank and he would immediately say, "You'r not think'en." That interested me but shortly after, he was all packed ready to go back to Detroit.

He had his barracks bag all packed and was waiting for a truck to pick him up along with the other boys. So I went over to him and asked him, "Heavy, would you tell me how you do this? I have my five dollar bill, my monthly wage." I said, "I'll give you my five dollar bill if you tell me how you do it." And he said, "I could tell you but you wouldn't be able to do it anyway. But think of one of these barracks." I think there was about eight barracks there. And so I was thinking of number six barracks. And he said, "Now think of one of the windows in the barracks." I was thinking, "Third window from the end." And he said, "You're thinking number six barracks. Number third window from the end." And he told me that, exactly what I was thinking. That taught me something.

So I had met some beautiful people. Some of my best friends. Erwin Elmo was one of them. And he'd have me play'en checkers with him all the time. Sometimes I'd win and sometimes he would win. And then I found out he was the checker king of the country. He was the champion of Michigan. And he knew every move on the board. And he let me win once in a while just so we could play together.

One time, another champion came from somewheres. The officers let them have a day off and they gave them a room with a table and a couple chairs. And those two played all day. That night I asked them, "Who was the winner?" and he said, "The one who started. The one who made the first move would win." That was as close as they were. He said that back home he didn't have anyone to play with and he'd have a piano chair and he would turn the board back and forth and he would play against himself. That's how he learned all the moves that there were on a checker board. A remarkable man and one of the greatest men I know of. Except my buddy, Bill Davis from Marian. They use to call him Crummy. His heart was made of gold. He was just one of the nicest people you could imagine. So him and I would buddy together a lot. He had a car and he would take us home on weekends, once in a while. So I'd ride home with him and stay overnight at his house. And he'd bring me home that evening. So I did meet some beautiful men. Floyd Collins was a sergeant there and he was Greek. He looked like it, a perfectly built man. And he got in a car accident and was killed there.

I Quit the CCC

I got notice one day that my father passed away. It hit me hard and I just started out through the woods. Run'en as fast as I could. One of the lieutenants caught me and brought me back and got me a truck to take me to the railroad station to take me home and instructed me, "to take over", and do what I could for the rest of the kids. Which I did.

Eventually the jobs started pick'en up a little bit like I said. Pontiac and Yellow Cab started calling back the men. And this was in Flint and Detroit. I went to Detroit to see if I could get a job. I quit the CCs. I think I was there 28 months. Of course I didn't have money. I tried to get a job at Ford's and there would be a line-up waiting at the gate. He would choose a few men and send the rest of them home, and tell them to come back the next day. But I could never get up to this gate, to the man. He had a little hut there where he would choose the people to be called into work. No matter how early I would get up there would still be a line there ahead of me. I guess they were there all night. It never dawned on me that was what they were doing. But they were old timers and well skilled, only they had been laid off.

So this man at the gate called me over one time and said to not waste my time, he said, "You'll never be hired here." So I took off looking for something else. I'd sleep in the rail way station. It was hard sleeping there because the benches had arm rests. You couldn't stretch out. The keeper there wasn't very friendly. And for food I'd go to a restaurant and wash dishes and for breakfast. I couldn't even have a cup of coffee until I washed a whole night's worth of dishes: a big sink full. Then I could have pancakes and a big slap of pork sausage. All I could eat, which was sufficient for the day with a candy bar or something.

Sometimes in the lobby of a hotel, sometimes there would be a chair there and I would sit in a corner until they would catch me and kick me out. Sometimes I made it through the night. So it was rough going. While I was in the CC camp there were a couple guys that were boxers. There was Pete Angelo and his brother and I was interested. They helped us by teaching us how to use the punching bags and the exercises that went along with boxing and the road work that we had to do to stay in condition. I still do it. The exercises helped me a lot through my life. But one of the boys that I was to box his name was Jolly and I figured he'd be a push over. But he wasn't. He used my head for a punching bag and before I could even get organized he broke my nose and gave me a black eye. I had to quit that. I figured it wouldn't pay off. I'd go into something else.

Saw Mill Work

Like I said before, I quit the CCCs. Before I left, I asked them for references and they were very generous with good references for me; a tractor operator and of course a cook and truck driver and all the other things I had done there. So I could see I couldn't get a job in the factory so I went out in the country to a saw mill and I showed this to the young cowboy. He wore cowboy boots and a black cowboy hat. It was on a farm, he had this mill on his dad's farm. His dad and other brother were farming the land. This fellow had developed a lumber business. And he would cut lumber for packing the car bodies for Henry Ford. He'd get contracts. He bought a little Caterpillar tractor so because I was a tractor operator in the CCCs, I think that helped me get a job there.

And during the weekend when the mill was shut down, I would take this tractor and plow for the farmer, his dad. And he would pay me extra. I had a shack there that I lived in. It was a shack that they would pull into the woods and use as a cook shack. It was portable. It made good living quarters for me. It had a stove. I took some sand and scrubbed the floors until they were white. It had a cupboard and he brought me a bunch of dishes. Of course I had plenty of wood to burn. I enjoyed that.

I'd go to town once a week to pick up some groceries. Eventually I earned enough to where I thought I could buy a car. So I hitch hiked to Detroit. It wasn't that far, about 20 miles to Detroit. The name of that town was Fenton. There was a Ford garage there. They were repairing Ford cars and selling them. Oh, there was one beautiful roadster. It was all painted up nice. I wanted it but he wouldn't sell it to me. He said, "It had a buyer." They had a coup there. Kind of a shaggy coup. Wasn't very good look'en but they'd sell it to me for $30.00 dollars. So I gave them $10.00 down and I drove it home. Then I was supposed to pay $10.00 a month but they actually wanted $10.00 a week! I didn't realize that.

I saved the money and they came to repossess the car but I had most of the money already. And they said, "If you get laid off you can come and work it off at our place. We're running a

32

garage there and you can come and help us out. You can pay the car off that way." They were quite liberal with me but I paid it off anyway, and fixed it up. And then I had transportation, which was pretty good for me.

We would go out into the woods and cut elm trees and then trim them up and make them into logs and then skid them into a pile. When we got enough we would get the saw going. I was working with Grandpa Jones and he had his own pick up. His saws and axes were sharp. You could shave with um. We'd go to the woods. The first day, oh, I was bushed. And an old cowboy asked me, "How did you make out?" I said, "He worked my butt off." And he laughed and he said, "Old Grandpa? He couldn't do it." He said, "He was riding the saw. And making you do all the work." I didn't know what "riding the saw" meant. But anyway I accused him of it the next time. He said, "Well, your work'en too fast and I can't keep up so I had to push down on the saw to slow you down." But anyway, I learned.

This winter time we sawed down one elm tree and it split and it was chucked full of honey combs. And I had a 12 quart pail there. I filled it up full for myself and he must have had two or three pails full. I don't know all what he did with his. I took it home and melted it. I put it on the stove and heated up that honey. I then run it through a sieve and I had quarts and quarts of honey there for most of the winter. And it was good honey too.

Working in a mill like that there's always danger. One of the things, when we had enough logs to start the sawing I'd have to ride a carriage. The carriage meant the contraption that went past the saw carrying the log. And this was a saw, oh, I'd say, six foot, seven foot or maybe eight foot across and that thing would just sing. It was sharp as a razor. And this log would be clamped in what was called, "dogs" in one end and the other. And it would run pass this saw and it would cut off a slab and then these dogs would have to be released and the log would have to be turned on this flat side. Then they would cut another slab until they had a nice square piece of log. Then they could just slice it like slicing bread; one slice at a time. But somebody had to be on the carriage to unhitch that first dog. And that was me.

And I had to ride past this saw. And the carriage went pretty fast. And if I made one slip and fell against the saw, then that would have been the end of Walt. And I didn't have good shoes. They didn't have any clogs in them and it was slippery too. So I always dreaded that but I always was nominated to ride this thing. Them days you couldn't say, "No" to the boss. If you didn't like it you could just walk off the job. He'd put somebody else on. So that was a ticklish part of sawing.

It was one time we were loading a tractor onto a truck and we laid a couple planks so the tractor could ride up on these planks. And the planks were laying flat and the tractor was up on the dock and it had to ride on these planks. And the truck was a little bit higher then the dock. And someone had set a cant hook on the end of the corner of this truck. One end was resting on the end of this plank. When the tractor hit the plank it catapulted the cam hook and none of us seen it go up. I don't know how high it went up. But it come down. Bang!! If it ever hit one of us on the head, it would have been the end of us. But those kind of things would be happening in spite of everything. Or sometimes we would be using a lath for turning out cant hooks and other things and sometimes the tool would hit a knot and this piece of material would fly out of the lath and going about 100 miles an hour. Around and around; that thing would fly up around the ceiling of the building and come crashing down in front of us. That's another thing.

In the camp next to us, there was some of those, "good ol'boys". And they was always joken around and they were coming home from the woods riding in the back of the truck. It didn't have a solid box, just a couple beams to roll the logs up on. They were riding on those beams and they had a log chain with them, laying there. And one of the jolly boys, he hooked the chain around a man's head. He had his back to him. He was joke'n around. Not meaning any harm. He hooked that chain around his head. At that very moment the rest of the chain, slid down and one end got under underneath the wheel of the truck and it jerked this poor man's head off. But it was all done in good clean fun and I am sure he would understand.

Tape 2, Side B (Series 1)

Singing: *Johnny Crack Corn*

Construction with Kid Brother Ted

In my cook shack, I use to like to pick up cans of soup. And my favorite was turtle soup. And I under stood there were several kinds of meat in there. So I figured I'd get all my vitamins and minerals that way. But this time, I was in a hurry and I didn't heat it. I thought maybe I could just eat it as it came out of the can. It was cold and I started eat'en it cold. It was turtle soup and it tasted like swamp. I could taste the swamp in it. It spoiled my taste for turtle soup which I had liked so well.

This farmer he had a daughter. She was going to college and of course she would spend her time on the farm there where the saw mill was. So once in awhile she would invite a couple of us to the house to eat some ice cream, chocolate milk or something, just for the heck of it. Her mother had a hired girl and she was just a teenager. And the two girls would chum together. They'd play ball all the time. I'd be out there working on something and that ball would come flying toward me and I would pitch it back to them. After a while that darn thing would come flying toward me again. Finally this girl said, "Don't go throwing it back. Wait till they come after it." So then I wised up what was going on. So this hired girl would come over and get acquainted.

And so we were going out together that summer. That whole summer we kept company. But she wanted to get married real badly and she was so young. She may have been older then she looked. I never did find out how old she really was. But she looked very young. I treated her like I would one of my sisters. She was good company and we would go to a movie or different places. But finally when she found out I wasn't about to get married, she talked with her dad about it.

I was at her house one time and he asked me about my thoughts on marriage. He said, "War is coming and if you get married now you probably wouldn't get drafted. And you could live upstairs in my house." He was giving me a hint but I said, "No, I'm not afraid of war." Which was a lie of course. But anyway when she found out I was…I really didn't have anything to offer at that time. And so when she found out I wasn't in the marri'an mood or marri'an kind…not able to marry her, she told me not to come around no more. So that ended that.

But anyway, my brother Ted came around one time. I came back from the woods and he was sitt'en there on the porch of my little cabin there. He was telling me about a job that was open, a construction job in Detroit that would pay 60 cents an hour which was really something. I was only getting 30 cents an hour where I was worken. But I didn't figure on that we would have to pay rent because my rent was free. And my work was steady. So what he was talking about was construction work. I had no idea what construction work consisted of at that time. I had a car and several checks maybe 30 or 40 dollars saved up and Ted had 7 dollars so we had quite a lot of money. So we ventured out. I took the job then. My old boss offered me a higher wage. An extra nickel an hour but I wanted to quit work with my brother anyway.

So we both went to Detroit. And we were supposed to meet a couple boys that instigated this job for us. They were working at Henry Ford's River View Plant. We were supposed to meet them at the gate, as they had left for the night. But we missed them and we didn't have their address. So somehow we sent a telegram to our brother Steve in Tustin. As it happened, he was in town at that moment and he received this telegram and he sent us a telegram right back. In the mean time, after we sent this telegram, I don't know where the heck we did it, because we didn't know where the post office was or anything. But we sat on a curb and waited a while and went whereever it was and the answer was there already for us.

So we met these two boys, Steve and Eddy Holga. They were from Reed City, a town next to us. We had known them for some time. We got this construction job. Iyeee, iyeee!! It was a job. Shovel and ditch digging and mostly it was swampy area near Henry Ford's plant at River View. And also we had to find a place to live. Not knowing the town, we wanted to live as close to the work as possible so we could walk to work. There was a street there called Salina Street. Home for…I don't know what they were, Syrians I think, olive skinned people with a kind of a hooked nose. They lived in that area. The whole street belonged to them. We eventually found a place. Somebody told us where to go. And there was a sheriff of Salina Street. He was a good look'en man. Big fellow. Very confident. He had a big white house on the corner there. Him and his wife were living there with a couple other boys renting a room.

Ted and I had a nice big bedroom and we had a quart jar setting on the table. We would put our food money in this jar. Down in the basement was a stove and a coffee pot: a place where you could cook and eat. So we would buy the groceries. Whoever would have the time would run over to the store and he would take the money out of the jar and put the change back in there. That's how we kept our records. We never locked the door. We never thought of locking the door. Finally when it was time to change the sheets, the lady would come up there and saw the door unlocked and a jar of money on the table she kind of hollered at us, "You don't do that in Detroit. You gotta keep the door locked and kind of watch yourselves a little bit."

We were work'en away, one of the various jobs things to do in construction. There was a crock about 30 inches high and inside and outside. It had to be cemented. The joints had to be cemented. So that's what we were doing this time. Well, the raw cement on bare hands was murder. It would eat the skin off. We didn't have any money for gloves. Well, we were work'en till we couldn't stand it no more and there on the side walk was a little stand and a man was in there selling newspapers and cigarettes and odds and ends. We asked him if he would sell us a pair of gloves on credit because we didn't get paid yet. We thought that we'd get paid weekly but it was biweekly.

And so we had spent all our money and now we had barely enough for potatoes and ketchup. So that's what we lived on for a week down in that basement. If we'd make coffee, we'd open up a can of Pet milk, well, all that milk would be gone when we came back next time. There were other bums down in the basement that weren't even working. And they'd be sleeping there. He allowed this because they were all his country men. So that's how we lived.

He finally built us a little box and put a lock on it where we could keep our milk and stuff, where it wouldn't be raided. He was a great man. So this guy not knowing us or anything, when he seen our hands, he loaned us a pair of gloves apiece, some bandages and some suave. All on credit. So first thing we did when we got our checks cashed was to pay him off and the next thing we did was go to a restaurant and order a square meal. We ordered a big one: a whole pie, a chicken each, mashed potatoes, dumplings. Those guys that were running this restaurant got suspicious of us. I don't think we looked very prosperous. But we had no idea of cheaten anyone. But anyway, they had all lined up; two cooks and owner were at the door so we couldn't run away. But when we walked over to the cash register and paid up on cash they said, "Come again, please come again." They liked this type of customer.

Ford Roadster, A Beautiful Thing

Eventually, I ran, accidentally into a garage that was selling these Fords. This one was a 1931 Roadster. Oh, it was a beautiful thing. It had a rumble seat and windshield wings and a well on each fender for a spare tire. That thing looked very nice except it didn't have a top. It had the bows but no covering on it. And so I traded my car for his. And only about twenty dollars difference but twenty dollars was twenty dollars back then. And then accidentally I ran into someone from the old country.

He looked at that car and he said, "I'll make you a top and I'll also make you some side curtains for $50.00." And I said, "Ok." And I left the car there for a couple of days. When I went up there to get it back, I couldn't believe it. It had a tan colored roof and side curtains. It was trimmed to make the car look sporty. Everything was perfection. He was a master. A master tent maker and you know…when I think now…I couldn't have been that lucky all the time. It had to be Spirit looking after these affairs for me. Over and over these things would happen. I didn't know the guy or anything. I just run into him. And he done me such a marvelous job. Well that made a *real* car out of it. And I hung on to it for a long time. Eventually my brother bought it from me and he used it for a long time. It was a beautiful look'en job.

And we lived in this Salina Street and later on, when the boys found out where we lived they were telling us that it was a very dangerous place. No one dared to go in there. No gringos. No white guys because they would get mobbed but liven with this Sheriff, we were protected. And my car was never touch. It was an open car. Anyone could have got in there and took off with it. Nobody ever touched anything. We would go walking through there, day or night and we felt absolutely safe as if we were in our mother's arms.

Everyone was so scarred of the sheriff. He was a Pistol Pete any way. He carried his gun and once in a while he would get jollying around with the guys on the street and pull it out and aim it at their head and they'd be squealing, lifting up their arms, cry'en. They'd be so scarred. He'd have them kind of terrorized, I think. Because they did as he told them. We were absolutely safe as long as we were living there.

Saving Eddie's Life

There was a wrestling arena there too. We go there and watch the wrestling. And one time, the Polish people found out where we lived and they were horror stuck. And they rented us a palace on Eugene Street, which was a Polish neighborhood where we would be "safe". So we moved over there. And next morning my car had been broken into. I had a clock that was imbedded into a rear view mirror; they couldn't take it out so they just broke off half the review mirror and took it. I didn't feel that safe anymore.

So the job was ok but the problem with construction was that it would always come to an end. Building was finished or whatever we were making would get finished so there would be an interval before you could get something else. Usually the money that you'd saved up would be gone then. By the time you started another job. This Eddie that was from Reed City, one day my brother Ted was working on a man hole, he was cementing it up. Farther down toward the river was another manhole. It was the last one before the crock ran into the Detroit River. At the end of the crock was a steel pipe and it went way out into the river somewheres.

Well, we were working on our manholes, finishing then off and Eddie was inside this pipe and he was cementing the joints. Same thing we were doing before, only this time he was in there. He was quite a long ways into this pipe. Then somebody opened the valve and turned the water on without telling any of us. And this water, come pouring past Ted and he looked down and he saw Eddie swimming and there was an air space at the top of this pipe and he was just a-goen'er. The water was carrying him, really. And it went so fast that it went right by the manhole and he couldn't stop. And lucky that I was at this other manhole and Ted yelled to me, "Eddie is coming through." So I jumped down into the water and I braced my legs to form a screen. And when he come by me, he hit my legs and I was able to fish him out of there. So we definitely saved his life because if he had gone past my manhole, he would have gone into a steel pipe and it would hurl him somewhere deep into the river. And that would have been the end of Eddie.

Buried Alive

Another time we had, somebody had goofed, like they always do. They had poured a floor in a factory, and they needed to lay another pipe in there, underneath this floor. So they cut a hole in this floor and made a tunnel; just a little tunnel about three feet high. They tunneled way back to where the pipe begun and then laid this new pipe in there somehow. And then it had to be backfilled. The only way it could be done...we had some candles and we would light them and stick them to the walls of the tunnel. Well, they gave me the job of carrying the dirt and packing it back to the back end of this little tunnel. The tunnel was about 50, no not that long: 25 feet maybe. Maybe 30 feet. They had one guy throwing dirt down into this hole and I would fill up my buckets and carry it back past these candles, the only light there was. And I'd pack the tunnel.

And I was working there almost all day and this time I came back to refill my buckets and the hole was full of sand. It was filled up. Some boys up above had came along with shovels. They had just finished their job and came by this one guy throwing dirt down into the hole. He was kind of a new man and he forgot that I was down in there. And he asked them if they would help him fill up his hole. He said, "I was throwing dirt in here all day and I can't seem to make any headway." And being obliging, they all got around there and they filled that hole up. So when I come back to the entrance of the tunnel, I couldn't hardly breathe and the hole was filled with sand. I tried to dig my way up but they were pouring sand in faster then I could dig my way out. So them lights begin to be going out. There wasn't that much air in there. The only thing I could think of was, I stuck my hat at the end of my shovel handle and I worked it up through the dirt and they could see my hat there at the end of the shovel handle. My brother Ted was one of the guys there. He recognized it. So they dug me out of there. But what would of happened if I hadn't been able to get that shovel handle up through the dirt? They would have packed it down and poured cement over it and wouldn't have even known where I went.

That new guy said, "Well, I knew there was a man down in there but I thought he went out the other end." That was his excuse.

We'd seen many tragedies happen there. One of them involved a union steward, a nice young chap. We had completed a five story building. There was duffle on top of the roof and we were throwing it down, clearing it. The steward was carrying several planks on his shoulder and he just shoved them off the roof, but there was a nail in one of them and it hooked onto his coat and those planks took him along. And he was killed. He fell five stories down. There was gravel down there and slag cement.

Another boy was climbing a derrick. A derrick was hauling cement up there and I was coming in with a little buggy to pick up the cement and I saw him climbing. I guess it was a homemade affair and the boards were nailed up there for a ladder and this boy was carrying some stuff and all of a sudden I didn't see him any more. He never reached the roof. He never climbed onto the roof. I looked down and he was laying down there. He had slipped or the ladder broke or something. There were about five guys were shoveling gravel into a mixer that was elevated up that derrick and they were so engrossed in their work that they didn't do nothing. He was laying there and they kept right on a work'en. Finally, somebody from the street recognized that there was a tragedy there. I don't know how badly the boy was hurt or if he was killed or not. I don't think he was killed.

There was always chains braking or the shovel would slip or the clutch would slip, they were digging ditches with it and that think would come fly'en toward our heads. Constantly there was danger. This one time at the Burrow typewriting plant, they had built a chimney. A nice round chimney. It went way up into the sky. And Ted was working right underneath it and I was on the outside of the building helping a welder weld his pipe. I was digging bell holes for him and Ted came walking up and he said, "They want you to quit for the day." And I said, Well, I'm not finished yet."

He said, "yah, but there was a tragedy." I said, "What happened?" And he said, "The foreman that had built the chimney had come over with his daughter and her girlfriend. There was no one working as the chimney was finished but the cables still ran up the chimney on the inside. That's how they would hoist the material and the workers would go up there. There was a platform at the top of this chimney and the friend of his daughter wanted to go up the platform. So they got somebody to run this donkey engine and the foreman and girl went to the top to view the country side from the top of this chimney. And they did and then when she got a hold of the cable, there was a nail keg only about a foot across, if that, it was full of cement and the cable was running through it and you had to stand on this nail keg and hold on to the cable to go up or down and she stepped up on this nail keg.

I don't know what happened but she let go and she fell all the way down the chimney and killed herself, of course. And he got a hold of the nail keg and rode part way down and then something happened and he let go and fell. He spoke to the people. He said, "Good bye boys." Then he died. Both of these people died. So usually when something like that happens, they stop work for the day so everyone's nerves will cool off. So there wouldn't be anymore tragedies for the day.

So winter would come and jobs would slack off for the winter and we would usually head back out into the country. Back home around Tustin. There would usually be something to do. There would be Christmas tree cutting. Or whatever a person could get a hold of, maybe working in the stables somewheres taking care of horses. But I wanted to stay over in town like everybody else did. And so my brothers all left for the country and I stayed there. I'd get a little job there even in the fall. But not very much and I had to pay rent. Mrs. Marshon had a boarding downstairs in her big house and the cheapest room was a coal bin there.

One of the guys that we were worken with, he was a little fellow from Canada, we called him, "Frenchie". Though he was small he put in a tremendous amount of work for a little guy so he was never wanting for a job. But this time he was whitewashing the basement for his room and board and I ran out of money so he let me in and I would sleep with him and he always had a pot of soup on. It was tomato soup with macaroni in it. So we always had something to eat. He would add tomatoes or more macaroni as needed but then Mrs. Marshon came down there and caught me sleeping in his bed and she kicked me out. She said, "Three dollars a week or out you go!" And in them days they didn't have any heart so she kicked me out in the snow and I walked a round and couldn't find a job of any kind. So I'd come back and the door would be locked but he would open he window and I could slip in for another nights sleep until finally she caught me again and kicked me out with a warning, a stern warning not to come back. But a truck driver with a good heart also lived there and he only slept 3 nights a week at her place and the other nights at the other end of his route. So he gave me the key to his room and I was, like a fool, I slept too late. I should have gotten up early but I didn't and she caught me in his room sleeping. She gave me another lecture.

But as luck would have it, while walking down the street, I met Lou. He worked with us on different jobs and he says, "I got me a job. Why don't you come with me as my helper? And then you can work too." Oh man! That was a godsend to me. So I went to work with him and he was mostly laying up manholes. He was very good at that. It is mostly brick work. He would have me handing him bricks and mortar and when the job was finished on a manhole, I'd get a gunny sack and wipe I all down and clean out the inside and then go to the next one. I was working pretty good there. It was an Italian crew. The foreman was a kind of wild guy and he was afraid for his own job, so he worked his men real hard.

Short, Life-time Employment

But then a union man came over and he wanted some money. These unions were starting up and I had never heard of unions before but now they were coming in there. And he had little buttons. For five dollars he would give you a button and you would put it on your hat and you would be good for one month. The next month the button would be a different color. So he demanded five dollars from me but I told him that I wouldn't pay him. He said, "Why?" and I said, "Everybody else is getting a dollar an hour and they are paying me only seventy five cents." And he said, "Can you prove it?" I said, "Yah, I got all my stubs in the house."

And I used the envelopes, I'd glue a bunch of envelopes together and I could put a date on them and I always put my check stub in there. So I had all my check stubs from the time I started working. And he says, "Come on. We're going to headquarters." He had a big limousine. I didn't even know we had a headquarters. But I was surprised. We drove to the headquarters and it was a quite big office and there were several secretaries there and they were all pounding their typewriters and everybody was busy scurrying around. I couldn't imagine such a thing. And he told them, "I'm from the union and you haven't been paying this man a dollar an hour like you were supposed to. And if you don't square it up, I'm going to close you down." And he was very tough with that mafia gang. I was amazed.

Apparently the union superseded the Brotherhood. Anyway they said, "Ok, ok, we'll take care of it." And this one guy came over to me and started talking real nice. He had a nice suit on and tie, a white shirt. And he was telling me it would be very hard for us to go back to the beginning and square it up with you like that. He said, "How would it be if we gave you a life time job with our firm?" Wow! I never had such a deal in my life. A life time job?! Oh, yes, I grabbed it. And he said, "Ok?" to the union Rep. Who replied, "I don't care as long as he's satisfied."

So they sent me back on to the job, this time paying me a dollar an hour, but then I noticed that when a derrick needed greasing and that required climbing way up high on the derrick, on a boom, and then you had to grease and oil the pulleys, I would be the one who would be sent up there. If we would be working underneath the railroad track in a tunnel, a train would come by and dirt would sift down my neck, I would be the one underneath these tracks. On a busy highway, I would have to be the one to go out on the busy highway. They wouldn't even put warning signs for me. And finally one of the men, an older person, he came to me and said, "The foreman has orders from headquarters to kill you. And if he doesn't kill you by accident then he's going to create an accident where you're going to die." So he says, "You're young yet. You can go out and find yourself some other job." He said, "I would recommend you get out of here while you are still able."

So I listened to him. I had a little money saved up then and this sheriff that we use to live with on Salina Street, he was a foreman for Henry Ford and he promised us if we ever saved up $50.00 and gave it to him, then he would get us a job at Henry Ford's factory, building cars, which was our dream! And he was running the Green Leaf Bowlers, a big machine there and he said, "You tell the guy at the gate that you had worked on Green Loaf Bowlers before and he will send you to me and I will show you how to work it." That sounded good.

So I went back to Salina Street, and I went over to this sheriff's house and he wasn't there so I went into the basement where the bums were living, and they knew me, so I asked for the Sheriff and they told me where he was, several blocks away in an old lady's bedroom. And I couldn't figure out what he was doing there, so I went up there. And he was cleaning his guns. He had them spread out all over the bed. And I asked him, "I got the $50.00 can you get me that job at Fords?" And he said, "Golly, I don't know if I have a job there myself." He says, "The union came in and they fought with Henry Ford." We used to see these police come in on horseback with long clubs and all these people standing around with literature in their hands. These police men would scatter them out and the police were working for Henry Ford and the other guys were union men.

And there were 15,000 men working in that factory and they'd have to pay the union $15.00 a month, apiece at that time. Can you imagine the money the union would make if they could take over the membership? So they fought hard and the Sheriff was telling me, "I was backing up the Ford cars and they threatened me and threatened my wife. I had to take my wife and child and hide them out in the country. And I'm hiding out here upstairs in the attic." He said, "I don't know if I have a job there but maybe things will cool down later on. You come and see me later." I could see it was a touchy situation there.

You got a Gun?

One day, we use to go to Salina Street, there was a wrestling arena, I think I mentioned it before. So one day I took Eddie, he was still around from Reed City, and him and I went to the wrestling matches. And coming back, we didn't drive, we took a street car. And it was a strange situation there. I can't quite describe it. But it was like a black hole. The street cars were running down below and there was like another street higher up and you'd have to go down stairs to the cars. There was a platform, then the rest of the stairs would continue down to where the street cars were. It was night time and usually the stairs were well lit but this time I noticed that there were no lights there.

So Ed and I started down the stairs and got to that first platform and we noticed a group of guys standing around there and then when we looked up, there were a group of guys upstairs too. And we were bottled in between the gang. They had a trap set for anyone who came down those stairs. I saw what was going on, so I whispered to Eddie, "You keep your hands in your pockets." Then outloud I said, "You cover me and I'll go downstairs and then I'll cover you." We had our overcoats on and I put my hands deep into my pockets and made out like I had a gun. And I walked right through these guys and put my back against the wall and I said to Eddie, "Ok, I got you covered come on down." And one of these hoodlums came up in front of me and said, "You got a gun? You got a gun?" I said, "Try something and you will find out."

46

Tape 3, Side A

Harmonica playing, _"Camp Town Races"_

Winter Work on the Farm

I use to drive around I had this little car now. Sunday I'd ride around and see what I could see in Detroit. And I heard this music coming from this building. It was out in the country and was a good sized structure. So I went in there to see what it was and it was a roller skating rink. And oh, it was so nice. I never seen one before. Oh, so nice. These kids would go around and around and around to this music. And they had white roller-skates and a short red dress or blue dress. They looked so nice. I figured I use to ice skate and it couldn't be much different. So I rented me a pair of skates and I went out there. Oh, man! My feet were going in three different directions at the same time. I'd want to fall on my back and fall forward. Lucky there was a hand rail there and I hung on to this rail until I could get my balance and gradually I started skating a little bit. More and more until I could stay up on my feet. So I'd go there once in a while. Well this time, Steve and Ted and Eddie Olda and Steve Olda were still with us. We were all together yet. And it was Sunday and they didn't have any where to go, we'd be driving around singing, "40 bottles of beer on the wall. Take one down and pass it around." And I drove over on the way to this building. I didn't tell them what it was. I acted ignorant. I said, "Let's see what is going on." We went in there. Oh, they were amazed. They were wondering, "Could we skate?" I said, "Go ahead. We'll see. Can't be much different then ice skating." They said, "you first...you first" so I put my skates on. I kind of wobbled and staggered there for a minute then took off skating. I said, "Awh, it's no problem at all." Boy! They couldn't wait to put their skates on. All four of them jumped on to the floor at one time. They were gonna skate like professionals. I never saw such a chaos. One guy would fall forward and all the stuff in his pockets would fly all over the floor. And the girls would jump over him. Then the other guy would fall backwards on his back and the same thing happened.

And I got a pretty good laugh but they got kind of suspicious that there was something fishy about the whole thing.

Anyway, it got to snowing and Mrs. Marshon she was getting too fierce, kicking me out so I decided I'd go back up North to see what I could find for the rest of the winter. And I had been working for some farmers the year before, cutting corn. And they didn't pay me. They didn't have any money at that time and I just let it go. But back in Tustin on my dad's farm, Steve and the girls were holding down the place, Nellie and Mary. I drove over there to see them and Nellie (she calls herself Ann now) and Mary said they were running low on potatoes and stuff so I drove over to this farmer and I asked him, "I don't want money but do you have some potatoes and stuff that I could take instead?" He was very glad and said, "Yeah, we got number two potatoes. They are good sound potatoes we'll sell them for fifteen cents a bushel. He gave me 3 bushels which was forty five cents and a half a bushel of turnips and a half a bushel of carrots, some bacon, some butter. Anyway he gave me about three dollars worth of stuff and then seventy five cents in cash. The car was a sagg'en.

The little Ford Roadster, and I got it all loaded up. I brought that load of food in and then I stopped at Anderson's store. Anderson wasn't there anymore but his brother Bob Anderson was running it and I told Bob, I said, "Offer them whatever credit they need for groceries and I'll pay you when I get some money. I got a job at Ted Anderson's farm so I'll see you later on." He said, "Fine." So I went to work for Ted Anderson. He was single and he had a pretty nice little farm. He had about 10 good milk cows and a big farm dog. And he was batch'en and he was a very lonely man. And I like to talk, so during our first breakfast, he was fry'en a tremendously large amount of pancakes. He sat it on the table in front of me then he started frying another big batch. I thought the first batch was for both of us but, no, for each of us and then he would fry pork sausage and Oh!, that smelled real good. He made good coffee too. Sometimes he would cook little potatoes. He had a cast iron kettle, on three legs, and he would cook these potatoes the night before and let them cool off, with their jackets on and then when he was done finished frying the pork sausage, he would peel these potatoes and drop them into the hot grease to brown them off. I never ate so good in my life!

Later on he told me that he would butcher out two pigs and he would grind all the meat into pork sausage filling two big crocks. This pork sausage was the best I've ever eaten. The flour for his pancakes had to be red wheat flour. That's hard flour. And if he couldn't find it in one town, he would drive to another town to find this red wheat flour. It sure was good. He would mix the batter the night before also. I think he put a little yeast in there and let it work all night. We ate very well. But then after breakfast, a story would come to my mind and I would start telling it and he wouldn't move.

Dad's Spooky Stories

As long as I was talking, he wouldn't move. He'd just sit there. And I'd finish one story and then relate something that happened in my life or something that my dad would tell me. Dad's stories were pretty good. I don't know how to evaluate them but he was telling as a kid one time he had a boy friend that he would go play with and as the times were …I imagine like our place…he'd go to the barn to sleep. It gave him more elbow room an and course more freedom and so he would go play late with the boys and then walk home and go to bed anytime, as long as he could get up in the morning to do his chores, which was mainly pasturing cows. They never had enough pasture so he would take them down the road and pasture them on either side of the road.

Dad as a boy, had epilepsy and it would throw him to the ground and really work him over. He'd be as if unconscious, then he'd pull himself together but it would take a couple days before he could come around and be normal again. This had been going on for a long time. This one time, he took a bottle with him, half full of water, and when he went past a cross road, he'd take a pinch of sand from each of the crosses and put it in the bottle. Then when he felt the epilepsy coming on, he would shake it up and drink it quickly. And it would ward it off. When he came home that night with the cattle, his mother, asked him, "Did you have your sickness today?" He said, "No, I did what you told me and it warded it off." She said, "What did I tell you?" And he told her this and she said, "No, I didn't tell you that. You must have dreamt it." So where ever it came from, he never had epilepsy after that.

Well, once again he was coming home late from playing with the boys and as he was approaching the barn door where he slept, he had a vision. It looked like someone kneeling down only it didn't touch the ground but it was above the ground, floating like and where its face should be, was covered with hair. And this being had its hands folded and was in that position, and it scarred my dad. He stood there scarred to death. Gradually, this thing began to move sideways and after a while, it cleared the door way and he made a dash for the door and covered up his head. He slept quaking until morning. In the morning he related this to his mother and two sisters and it was near a pig pen, where the two sisters would carry the food to the pigs. They were scarred to go out there now. My dad saw where he could have some fun. So he took a bed sheet and hid himself in the pig pen. And he waited. He figured, sooner or later they would have to feed these pigs. He was going to scare them. Mother saw that the kids were scared, and said, "I'll go with you." So the three of them were marching toward the pig pen carrying a bucket of pig food. When they got near enough, he jumped up and let out a yell with the sheet over his head.

The two girls abandoned the mother. They let out a shriek and headed for home. But she was the bravest of the three. She picked up the bucket and hurled it at his head. And then she took off for home after the girls. Well, he picked up the bucket and come home laughing, what a trick he pulled. But she gave him a grubben! She said, "I'm not beating you for the trick, but if that bucket would have hit your head it would have certainty killed you." So when he first told her of the vision, she said, "Oh, it must have been your uncle who had passed away. He must have wanted to relate a message. But because you were so scarred, he wasn't able to talk to you." Well, I thought, when I heard this story, that if the uncle had actually showed up, she would have hurled that bucket at his head.

Anyways, as long as I talked, old Ted Anderson would sit there and finally, it would be getting close to dinner time and he's say, "Well, its getting too late to be getting out in the woods, this morning." He'd say, "Why don't you go throw some feed to the cows and horses and I'll get things ready and we'll go out to the woods after dinner. And get some work done." We weren't working. We had do some work because he didn't have any wood split up for the night. So we would saw down a tree and take a team of horses along and drag this log home. Then take a cross cut saw and saw it up the logs, stove size and throw it through the window into the wood shed. And that was our work for the day. And that went on day after day. I would have to take the cows out sometimes and water but he said, "Don't drive um. That's the dog's job." He'd get insulted if you took his job away from him." So I would release the cattle and the dog would take them, I don't know where, somewheres where there was a creek and it wouldn't freeze over.

He would take them there for a drink. When the cows had a drink the dog would obediently bring them all back to the barn. This one time, the dog forgot one cow and Ted came out there and talked to him, "Aw, you made a mistake." (He called the cows by name) You better go and get Daisy. You forgot Daisy." The dog kind of hung his head and went back and found Daisy and brought her back too. This dog was a Shepherd or Collie with heavy fur. There was a crack by the kitchen door and he would always lay next to the crack where he could get some air. He was warm with that heavy winter coat on. So he kept the wind from blowing underneath the door and at the same time he would stay cool.

Well this one time Ted was looking for Red Wheat Flour. He couldn't find any at the regular store so he had to go to Cadillac about 15 miles away with his Model T Ford to pick up the flour there. While he was gone, I started looking around at what he had there. He had cellar doors, so I went down to see what was in the cellar. It was a full barrel of apples. They were kind of drying out a little, but they were still good. So I took a bucket and brought these apples up and pealed them and quartered them and cut them up and made two thick apple pies. I browned them off real nice and they were on the table. When Ted come walking in, he spies these apple pies a big gleam came into his eyes. He then took a knife and cut one pie clean in half and shoved it over on his plate, sat down and ate it all. Then after that, whenever he would go anywheres he would always say, "And you stay home and make some pies." That was my job from then on.

Going to Detroit

Well…My brother Steve, he kept telling me about how I had some money coming. I said, "No, I've been paid." But no, there was one check that I did not get. I was at the farm house that night. I slept over. I was sleeping in my mother's bed. Like I said, she use to have these premonitions. And this time I had a premonition. It said, "Your check will come." That made me real glad because I did not know when I was going to get it or even if I would get it. I went to town and sure enough, that last final check from Detroit was there. That was the first time I had a premonition that my mother used all the time. Anyway, it had come to me.

So I was working for Ted, not working very hard. Winter was going by. My brother Steve kept telling me that I had some money coming to me. I kept saying, "No, I already got my check." But I kept hearing the same thing from other people. Well, what it was was unemployment. Apparently congress had passed it and those that were unemployed could get some money. And so I hitch hiked to Cadillac and went upstairs as directed and there was a guy there and asked me where I had worked. He then pulled out a big book with all the construction companies and he signed me up for unemployment. He then said, "Now you have to go find yourself a job. If you cannot find a job then come back here next week and put your name down." So that's what I was doing through out the winter. Going there putting my name down. Putting my name down. Twelve times I did that. Then one day Steve come. He had twelve checks for me. Twelve envelopes with twelve checks of money. Boy! I felt pretty rich. So I gave Steve a few of them. Then I went to pay Bob up; the grocery store man. It was not very much. I was surprised at that. They didn't get much groceries there. I don't think the girls got groceries but I think Steve was getting groceries for credit. I know I owed Bob some money because one time I was hitchhiking and he picked me up and ask me when I was going to pay the bill. So I knew there was a bill there but it wasn't very much. But anyway, I got squared up with him. Then I figured, maybe I would finish up. It was getting toward spring and there was more construction going on. And things would open up. So I figured I'd take a trip over to Detroit to check up.

Going to Detroit

In order to make a break with Ted... we were pretty close by then and he wished that I could stay through summer to work with him. But that wasn't my idea. My car was in his hay mow. Parked inside his hay mow on the top floor of his barn. So we rolled it out, poured some hot water on the manifold. It started. But it was only about a half mile where they didn't plow the road and the snow was, oh, at least 2 feet deep and I couldn't drive that thing. But I would put it in low gear and Mr. Anderson would sit on the radiator and drive a team of horses, hooked on to the hood of this car. So while the car was doing the best it could the horses were supplying the other power and we were able to get out onto the highway. Or to the road that was plowed. So I told him that I would come back to see him before I left. I went over and bought a quart of whisky. Good whisky. I figured that would keep him cheered up for a long time. So I came back and presented him with the whisky and I told him, "good bye." And I headed out for Detroit.

Well there still were no jobs to be had in Detroit. So I drove around the parameter there, through the farms. And stopped at a farm house and the people would ask me, "Are you an agent from Townsen plan?" In them days Townsen was running for president because of the depression and hard times he had a plan to bring prosperity back to the country. And his plan was, according to him, was to pass out two hundred dollars to each family. And they were to spend this two hundred dollars within one month in order to collect another two hundred dollars. And so I found all these farm families being in favor of this plan. When I would ask them, "how do you stand for Towson and his plan?" They would all smile and say, "You must be one of his agents. Come in for supper. We'll fix you up a supper." I found that was a good way to eat. So I would drive to different farms and invariably they would come up with this "agent for Towsen" idea if I asked them if they would vote for him or not. This one time this farmer, he was a bachelor too, well, he brought out a jug of wine. He poured me a good big schnapps and we had supper. He wanted me to stay and work for him. He had some apple trees there and he said we can trim apple trees and stuff like that until the snow blows, then we can work the farm. But I still wanted to work in Detroit, so I kept right on a-goen but this night I got caught out on the road with no place to sleep and there was a nunnery out there. It was a…I don't think they were Catholic nuns but they were nuns of some kind. They had big white bonnets and black dresses. A bunch of women. I asked if they had a place to put me up for the night. They said, "No." They didn't have any facilities but if I just go a short ways over the hill, there was a poor house there and they would put me up. So I went over to this poor house. I never was in one before, I was sort of curious to see what a poor house looked like. Sure enough, there it was. It was like a big army barracks and I went in there and there was a group of people in there talk'en and laugh'en. They seemed so happy and the place was so clean. The floor was spotless and the beds were made up and they were telling me, "Oh, good. We're glad you come. You have supper with us and then after supper, we're going to have a movie and we'll all enjoy this movie." So I did. Supper consisted of fresh bread and cabbage soup and potatoes and something. I don't know what but sufficient, plenty of it. And they bowed their heads and all said grace. Which was went a long ways with me and they put me up for the night in one of their little bunks there. I thought if I ever wanted to retire, I'd want to retire to a place like that. See a movie at night. Live with people, have company. But I had to go on.

Manna From Heaven

So I went deeper into Detroit still looking for work. This time I would buy a paper and sit on a bench and look at the want adds. And there weren't very many there really. Not the kind of job I could do anyway. Finally, there was one that caught my eye. It was a farm job and asked for someone to plow. Of course plowing was no problem for me. I did plenty of that for my dad.

And a strange thing was, the address was a city address. I couldn't figure it out but I went down and located it. It turned out to be a butcher shop. So I went in and talked with the lady there. She said, "Yes" they had a farm and needed someone to start plowing and to get things ready for spring planting. And I said, "OK." And we agreed on a price and she said, "We will drive over and you follow us. We'll take some food along." So she got about four or five pounds of hamburger, some bread and some other stuff and I followed her.

And yes, there was this farm. It looked pretty good. And there was an old man there and she called him, "grandpa." He was kind of looking after the place. Feeding the horses and some hogs there. So she introduced me and left. Well, next morning…these horses were in the barn and no one had been exercising them for I don't know how long. And they were raring to go. A big team of horses. I hooked them up to this plow and I set the plow as deep as I could and they would run. And I was plowing at a dead run, back and forth, back and forth. I don't think anybody ever plowed that much ground in such a short time like I did with them wild horses. But gradually-gradually, they tired out and they became more gentle. So I worked that day and went back to the house. The old man had boiled some potatoes and bread. That was out dinner. I worked a while there but it just didn't look good for me.

I didn't see any future there so I asked the old man, "Why don't you get out of here? I'm going to leave." He said, "Oh, they'll think that I drove you out." I said, "I don't care what they think." I said, "You can come along with me. I'll take you down to the poor house." He said, "Well, that's what they were threatening me with. If I don't work here they are going to put me in the poor house." I said, "Did you ever see a poor house?" He said, "No." But he thought it must be something terrible. I said, "That's a real nice place to live. There are people your own age there. Everything is nice and clean and you can work if you want to but you don't have to work any more." I said, "Let them put you in the poor house if they want to. Don't be afraid of it." I said, "But I'm going to go." So I fried up all the hamburger and had one more good meal yet and then I took off for Detroit.

Well then something happened. I don't know how Steve got a hold of me, my older brother. But he called me and said that he was in Traverse City and he was working in the Vern Baker rider academy and they needed another man and wondered if I would be interested. Well, that was like manna from heaven for me. And you know what manna from heaven is? Moses when he was traveling with his people through the desert and they had nothing to eat and the Lord sent him down bread from heaven. It was flakes like frost and they would pick it. It was very good. It tasted like honey. That's what I felt like when I received this call. So I accepted the job right there on the spot and headed right back to Traverse City.

When I got there I could see Brother Steve had it made. When he came to meet me he was wearing a white coat, trimmed in blue, the colors of the stable. There were two rows of horses one on each side of this fair barn. It was a fair grounds area. Then he showed me his quarters. It was one of the horse stalls. It had a stove in it and a floor in it. I think it was a tack room really. They had saddles, bridles and various blankets in there along with ropes. His quarters were this stall. It was an extra big stall. Two bunks. I could see right away that this was going to be a luxury apartment for us. There was a little kerosene burner. It had a top on it where we could keep a coffee pot. Wow! We were going to have coffee too! He invited me for some coffee and he had some ginger snaps that someone had left to feed the horse but he kind of by passed the horse and shared it with me. Mr. Burn Baker, the big boss himself, came up, and he was big. He was a former champion wrestler. He showed me personally how to clean a box stall, shovel out the manure and how to curry comb the horses.

So between Steve and I, we split the horses. I took half of them and Steve took half. We'd put them in a hitch for curry combing them each morning. We would brush them and comb out their main and tail and then redo their box stall, put fresh straw in it. Then put them back in and then get another one out. When we would get caught up and put a saddle on and take them out in the riding rink and exercise them. It was really a pleasant job. We'd get meal tickets. That's how we would eat. We'd go to the restaurant and get a cheese sandwich or something for dinner.

Once in a while Mrs. Baker would invite us to the house for food. Sometimes Mr. Baker would join us at the restaurant and buy us a bottle of beer to go with our spaghetti. We were living royally. It was very exciting because there was always someone coming to ride or learn to ride.

First I had to teach myself but it didn't take me long to learn to post and the basics of it. Ordinary we would take the green riders to the rink and close the gates so the horses wouldn't run away. We'd get them started. We didn't loose too many of them. I knew I did one. We had two nurses from the hospital there. They were hard nuts and wouldn't listen to anything I told them. So we rode a few times in the rink but they didn't want to stay in the rink. They wanted to get out in the trail. I had an old pokey horse, I don't know why, but they had the good ones. We started out on the trail and the horses were anxious to run. And the girls didn't know how to control them so they just kept going faster and faster. My old plug couldn't keep up. There wasn't much I could do. So this one could ride a little. She stayed on her horse but the other one kept being thrown forward onto her horse's neck. Finally she was riding this horse with her arms around its neck and her legs around its neck. I don't know how he could run with her but he was running. I just couldn't catch up to them. I could just barely reach his tail with my hand. But my horse couldn't go fast enough. Hers was going full gallop. Finally gradually, she slid around underneath her horse and let go. The horse ran right over her. I went and caught the horse but I was scarred to even look at her. I thought the horse had trampled her.

But the horse never laid a hoof on her. She was rolling over to one side and got herself under a tree and sat down. Her partner came over and consoled her and I finally got her to get back up on the horse to go home. This time they stayed behind my horse. I could control them then. We got them back to the barn safely. But you know, the girls didn't want another lesson. They never came back. Baker was wondering, "I wonder why they don't come?" But we didn't enlighten him.

Steve and I worked there a long time. He liked us pretty well. We became good horsemen after that. We taught a lot of people how to ride. Eventually we thought we could improve on our work so we quit him. Quit Mr. Baker and his ridding academy. We then had various jobs. Steve went to work for Mr. Baker's dad who was running a lumber mill in a deep dark woods. And I was picking up jobs at different farms. This one farm was a pretty good farm. It had several milking machines and several nice cows. Nice hay, alfalfa hay. It was so green it looked like you could make salad out of it. It was put up outside in stacks. This was winter time and jobs were hard to pick up at that time. So I'd take anything I'd get.

This farmer would go load up this hay with a team of horses and a sleigh and take it to the barn area where he had a truck. We would put it on the truck and he would sell it. I don't know what they did with it, maybe made it into alfalfa pills or what. It was a really nice way to put up hay. I kept working for him. One of the things in the house, no matter how cold it was, the room I slept in was *ice* cold. My shoes would stiffen up so I could barely put my feet in them in the morning. He wouldn't let me crack the door open but he did have a feather-thick and it was great. Once it got warmed up, it didn't matter how cold it was outside. It was just comfy to sleep under. I had never slept under one before. Well, he had a little girl and boy maybe…in about early grade school. And I was amazed at how those kids would work after they came home from school. They would change cloths, get their sled, go to the wood pile, load it up and they would bring the wood and fill up the wood box. This wood box was unique. Half of it was inside the house and half of it was outside the house. So they would load it from the outside and then go inside and pick the wood up to fire the stove. The heating stove and cooking stove were both wood burners. The lady was real nice. But this man, there was something physically wrong with him. He would get the shakes sometimes. And she would have to grab him and hold him until his shakes receded. Sometimes he would kind of go nuts, to tell you the truth.

This one time, I was loading hay, throwing it down from the mow on to the truck. He was down below stacking it. We both had pitch forks and he started antagonizing me very hard, insulting me in every way. And he was ready with the fork. He thought I would jump down and attack him. And he would have the fork ready so I would jump on the pitch fork. And I don't know if that would have given him jollies or what anyway I could see through that so I ignored him. I finished the work and next day he was alright again. But I didn't trust him. Then one day he wanted me to climb up on the windmill with him to help grease it or oil it or tighten something up. So I quit him.

Tape 3, Side B

Harmonica: *Oh Them Golden Slippers*

So that's what happened. Eventually I got in touch with Baker. He had moved out to Grand Rapids. He had a nice place there, started his riding academy there for some of the rich people. That particular club furnished him with a riding rink, barn, a house and everything. So he moved his horses there and promised me a job come spring. So that's how it happened that I started working for him again. And eventually my brother came along. His job in Detroit did not open yet. So him and I worked together for a while and it was great to be together again riding the horses. Different things would go on like parties and cook outs, clubs and so on which made it very interesting for us. Eventually, he was called back to his work in Detroit and I was there with Mr. Baker's son. We called him Bud. He was just a young fellow. Probably 14 or 15 but he was the best horseman I've ever seen.

This one time, Mr. Baker was having a horse show and he asked Bud to ride. Bud had a little bay pony that he rode and was his own. He could get his pony to go full gallop around the riding rink. When the horses would go his belly would just about touch the ground...full gallop and Bud would hang on to the saddle horn and jump over this horse, from one side to the other, one side to the other. He then would get up on the saddle and stand upright and ride Roman style, standing straight up. He was just a-go'ener. I never saw anything like that. I wasn't aware that he was so capable because he never showed off or anything. Ordinary he'd ride that horse at a gentle canter. That horse had a canter like you've never seen. Of course he was so use to riding it that it was like a rocking chair. The horse and boy were like one. And I noticed Mr. Baker would see him coming around the bend sometimes to the barn from riding out on the road, and Mr. Baker would get his camera. He would make him go out and come in again so he could take his picture. He says, "I never get tired seeing this boy riding." And it was a picture.

Well, this one time it wasn't so picturesque. I didn't know how serious this was. This horse managing. But there was a trail on the other side of a two lane freeway. Bud's horse refused to cross it. He had apparently had slipped on the cement and it scarred him and no matter what Bud did, the horse would not go across. So he brought him back and put him in the barn. For some reason he told his dad about it and his dad got furious, really angry. "You let a horse do that to you? Get your spurs on. Get your spurs on!!" So he made this boy put his spurs on and gave him a riding crop and he himself took his whip. This whip was like a buggy whip and when he cracked it, it sounded like a rifle shot. He could pick a bug off a horse's ear without touching him. So he said, "You better come along Walt."

So we go back to the road where the horse refused to cross. And ol'Mr. Baker got behind the horse with the whip crack'en. The horse still refused to cross so he would crack it again. And the horse was so frightened; the devil couldn't have frightened him anymore. The horse would get down on his knees and everything but it wouldn't help. And Bud was so scarred that the whip would get his own butt that he was leaning way over onto the horse's neck, as far away as he could get from the whip and spurring this horse. Between Bud and the whip they put him across the road. The horse crawled and half walked but he went across the road. So they made him come back and do it again several times. Then finally they put him in the barn. But I could see that I was working for a very hard man. Not someone to cross.

Yet, I did it. In ignorance and he didn't hold it against me. He had a horse it was suppose to be a jumper. These jumpers were supposed to go anywhere. Jump any kind of a jump-hedge, road, ditches or fences, whatever. And he was training this horse. His name was Red Wing. A big roan. One day, I was riding this horse down in a valley. And down in this valley I saw a bunch of wooden jumps. I hadn't been there before. So naturally I was going to try him. I put this horse over the jumps and he would jump them but after a while he got tired of it and he wouldn't jump for me no more. I didn't have any spurs or a crop or anything. In fact I wouldn't beat anybody else's horse. I never did. So I took him home and put him back in his stall and wouldn't you know, the next day some people come over to look at this horse and Mr. Baker brought him out and says, "Now this horse is a jumper and he will take any kind of jump." There was one jump there and he brought the horse up to this jump and the horse refused to jump. And so he says, "Well, I guess he's not feeling up to it today." And put him back in the barn and brought out some other horses.

So that night when we were eating supper he asked me, "Were you riding that horse?" I said, "Yea, I took him out and I found these jumps in the valley." "At first," I said "he jumped all right then he refused to jump just like he did for you. I brought him home and put him in the barn." And he says, "You undid hours of work that I did on that horse." So next day I saw him saddling this horse and he had his spurs on and a big heavy riding crop. He took this horse over to that hill and I tell you that horse jumped anything that came along. I know he could jump. We would put him in the riding rink sometimes at night to graze and we would find him in the garden the next day eating cabbages. And somehow during the night he would jump the fence that was at least five foot high. But he was capable when he wanted to jump but when he wanted him to do it, he would refuse. I knew Baker retrained him again. I don't know whatever happen to that horse.

Harmonica: *The Strawberry Roan*

There was this chestnut horse that Baker had. He was a young one, but he was vicious and Baker brought in a horse jockey that was suppose to be able to break horses but this horse threw him and the guy went home. No one ever road this horse till I got there. So he was in my string and I used a different tactic. I bought a box of lump sugar and I carry some in my pocket and every once in a while, I'd give him a couple of lumps. He got to looking foreword to it and eventually, there was a vacant barn pasture, away from the house and I would lead him over there, saddled and bridled. We'd get in there and I would lock the door then I would have him stretch out. I would put some weight on the saddle to have him get use to it.

Actually, these horses there kind of single minded. If they are doing one thing, they are not thinking of the other. So while I was getting into the saddle, I would give him another lump of sugar. And he let me sit there. And eventually, he let me ride him around on the in side of the barn. And I'd take him home. Clean him up. Give him some oats and he was a happy little horse. He started to gain weight. He was so nervous that he was skinny. I guess somebody told the boss about it and Baker asked, "Are you riding that horse?" I said, "Yea." He said, "Well, I gotta see it." So we went back there and he road another horse and when we got there he said, "I never saw anybody mount a horse any better then you did. Let's take him out." So we opened the gate and he just took off in a gallop. And that red cuss that I was on just followed and we took off cross country. We would jump logs and ditches. It felt like I was riding on a stack of pillows. I never had such a ride in my life.

Later on I told Mr. Baker how it felt to ride this horse and he said, "That's because his back hadn't stiffened up yet." So it felt like a bunch of pillows. But he was spooky, that horse. One night I was getting ready to go to town and I put on my new pair of jodhpurs, my boots and white shirt that I had special for that occasion. I had some money in my pocket. Then Mr. Baker came along and said, "I'd like you to take that horse out in a ring once." I said, "I'm all dressed up now to go to town. I hate to monkey with it now." He said, "Oh, I'll saddle him for you if you will ride him once. I want to see him in a ring." So we took him in a rink and what Mr. Baker did was to tight the curb chain him and I did not know he did that. This curb chain is very severe. If you tighten up on it, it can throw the horse backwards. And that's exactly what happened. The horse was kind of spooky anyway and when I got on him, he wanted to run. And I didn't realize, and I pulled back on the lines and he flipped over. And I just had to roll to get out of the way. If you get a ton or a half ton of horse on your chest, you're not going to feel too well. If you fall off, you have to roll real quick. I did not even know what happened to that horse.

He ran off a ways and Mr. Baker said, "We'll never catch him." But it wasn't so. His lines were down and he stood there like a rock. I went out there and picked them up. A couple days later I was riding him and he got spooked and before I realized it he headed for a wooden fence. He jumped. He didn't quite make it. He ticked the last rail with his hind leg and skinned it a little bit. When Mr. Baker saw it he said, "That horse will never show anymore." He wanted him for a show horse and they have to be perfect. And I asked, "Why?" And he said, "It will grow a lump on that ankle." I said, "Naw, I'll bath it in hot water and vinegar and it will be alright." I didn't believe it. But it was like he said and the horse developed a lump. "It won't hurt the horse any, as far as being a horse, but he won't show no more. He's not perfect." he said. I felt kind of guilty about it all so I asked him what he wanted for the horse. He gave me a price and we came to an agreement. And I bought that thing.

So this time, a couple ponies somehow they got out and managed to get out on the road. There's nothing more dangerous then a horse on the road. They will come out from the bushes right into the path of an oncoming car. When a car hits a horse somebody's going to get hurt. And I knew it! When I realized they were gone, I grabbed the first horse I could get a hold of. It was an odd looking thing. I don't know where Baker got it. But it had big hoofs, like a farm horse but he was just a pony in size. I grabbed that thing and I didn't even put a bridle on him. I just grabbed him like that. I had a short lasso in my hand and I drove him like that. Well, we took off after these critters. Well, I didn't know that this horse was a cow horse. He was trained to drive and cut and all that. He was chas'en these horses. They were off to one side along the fence and we had clear going on the road and we were gaining on them. They had to go around stone piles and brush. As soon as we got to where he could cut them off, that's exactly what he did. Without telling me about it. Man! I almost went on my nose. He cut right in front of them and cut them off and turned them around. So, we started off toward the barn.

I thought if I kept going fast then they wouldn't have time to think of some other thing to do. So I was driving them fast. We were going across a plowed field. Those darn horses...one went one way and one went the other way. So this cuss I was riding didn't know which one to chase so he put on the brakes and I into that plowed furrow. But he waited for me and I got back on. Finally got them things corralled but that night while we were eating supper, I noticed everyone was kind of snickering into his plate. Finally someone asked me, "Did you have a nice ride this afternoon?" And it seems like everyone seen me take that dive off that cuss and they sure gave me the raspberries. Even after I went to town, I got the same thing from the town's people. They knew all about it. I gota lot of raspberries from falling off that horse.

We had one horse his name was Sunday Blustery. He was probably the best jumper in the United States. He liked to jump. He was a rangy horse. He would walk up to the jumps and measure himself; all by himself. He would walk back and then he would jump over. Then Mr. Baker would raise the bar maybe 6 inches at a time. The horse would come measure himself, back off and then come running and jump over again. He would do that as long as someone was working with him. He was very valuable. He was also the best looking horse. So when Mr. Baker wasn't around I would get a Western saddle and put it on him. And a Mortin Gale and dress him up. Baker had some fancy equipment there for his horse. I'd dress the horse up and take him for a ride. I'd visit my friends with him. Show off a little bit. One time he got tired of me messing around and wanted to go home. He ran underneath the cloths line. I had to lay flat on his back to avoid being rubbed off. I can imagine what would happen if this horse come charging down the road all by himself with no body on him.

Anyway, one day Bud came to me and he said, "Walt, I hate to say anything but if my dad ever saw you riding that horse like that he will skin you alive." He was worried for me. I don't know if any one ever told Mr. Baker. They were pretty good about keeping quiet about those things. But one day there was an enormous amount of riders came. Every horse in the barn was saddled except Sunday Blustery. Somebody had to go with that gang or they would have gotten into trouble. Baker says to me, "We got Sunday Blustery there. You don't suppose you can ride him?" I said, "Well, I guess it would be alright." Of course he was the most sensible horse in the whole bunch and I knew it. Sunday Blustery lost his life in a fire and I still feel bad about him.

There was this time when the army Calvary used horses and they put on a training. They needed a lot of horses so they would pay $40.00 a month to rent the horses. So being enterprising Mr. Baker would get all the horses he could in the area and he would rent them out to the Army boys to ride. Those horses were kept in a corral and they would bite each other. They were always selecting the leaders so they would kick each other and bite. And they'd get skinned up pretty bad. Mr. Baker did not want to turn the horses back to their owners in that condition so his cure was to turn them out on the back pasture for a month or so as long as he could keep them. They heal up and calm down. That was most of the time that's how he would train horses that had been spoiled by too much training. He would just turn them loose and let them calm down for a couple months. That's all they needed.

Anyway these two horses came back. They were from Redding. They were big horses. Ugly looking. Big hammerheads. Two of them. And the Calvary men couldn't get anyone to ride them. They would throw them. And when they would throw them they would *really throw* um. They were mean devils. So we turned them out on the back pasture and eventually the owner wanted them back. Mr. Baker told me to go get um. I could have got on another horse and drove them back but I wanted to ride one of them. I thought it would be a great honor if I could ride one of them while the army boys gave up.

So I took some oats in a bucket and a lariat and went out there. My scheme was that while he was eating oats I would slip this lariat over his nose. I could hold him and then mount him and come riding in. This wild horse! I knew the other horse would follow him. But it didn't work out like that. That rope instead of going around his nose slipped around his lower jaw and he could pull a plow with his lower jaw so no matter how I hung on he'd pull me. Hanging on to a rope is a strange phenomenon. You can't let go when someone is pulling the other end. So we were running in this pasture and up ahead I see a tree. And I figured if I could go on one side of the tree and just wrap it around just one time I could hold him. I could mount him and ride him in. So we were headed toward this tree and I was about half way around it but the horse was more powerful then I was and he whipped me back around the tree. The rope cut a grove in the palm of my hands and it really smarted. So I had to go get a horse and bring him in the proper way.

Courting Time

Harmonica: *Oh Do Da Day*

Well, time goes on and this time I was driving through Grand Rapids on the way to Detroit. Usually I slept in the car. I had some GI blankets and pillows in the back seat. I took advantage of that rather then finding other places. But this time I was driving and stopped at this building. There was music coming from there. Polish music. And it was of course just a gathering place, club like. And somehow they let me in there. I ordered a beer and sat at this table. Looked the place over and it was just like on the radio. Those guys could really play. And everybody was doing the polka. Over in a booth sat a man with two girls. And I figured he didn't need two girls. I could see he was eyeing this one so I left her alone and I asked the other one if she cared to dance and she did. And awww, she just polkaed all around me. Well anyway there were these two girls and I danced with one and introduced myself. She introduced herself. (in Sophie's own voice on the tape recorder) My name is Sophia Mary Krystoff. I'm 21 years old and I love music and I love to dance.

Singing together, Billy Boy

I got a night job at Pantland Hotel in the laundry downstairs. That worked out pretty good because they would give us one meal there. It was a tremendous meal. It was a platter with a metal cover over it. Each of us received one of those platters for our lunch. It usually consisted of mashed potatoes, string beans, gravy and a couple big pork chops or a stake and rolls. Just a tremendous amount of food of which I ate every bit of it so I wouldn't have to eat the rest of the day. Maybe a cookie or something. It worked out good except I didn't have enough time to sleep. And also by then I was dating Sophie and she expected me to be there on time.

I remember this one day, I woke up and I was supposed to go to school that morning. I was going to riveting school at the time. I had slept maybe two hours after work as much as I could and I woke up and it was kind of dark and I was thinking maybe the sun didn't come up yet or maybe I had slept all through the day and it was getting dark. And I couldn't tell which was which. I walked out on the street; I thought I could then recognize if it was morning or evening coming on. But it was about the same amount of people on the street and they looked about the same. And I still couldn't figure out if it was morning or evening. And I didn't want to ask someone because they would think I was cuckoo. But then the sun peaked up over the hill and I knew I slept only two hours and not the whole night. So I was all right but many times I would tell Sophie I would be there at a certain time and she would be all ready and I couldn't make it.

She didn't know what was going on and she would blame me for being inconsistent. But she was alright. We would usually go to a movie and I would take her to dinner sometime. But it would take all my money so one day I had to confess to her, "I can't take you to dinner." I said. "I don't have that much money." We would stop in for a hamburger or something. So she said, "Well, why don't we go more on picnics. I love picnics and I can always fix a picnic lunch." And she would raid the pantry. Her mother was an excellent cook. She would make porogies and they were extra large and apple pies that were extra thick. Man, when she fixed lunch, it was really a lunch. We had a great time. Sophie didn't know how to drive yet. I let her drive my Pontiac. I had a Pontiac coup at that time. She was doing good. We were on a side road. Then someone tried to pull us over. They would drive along side of us and motion for us to get off the road and stop and then they would get behind us again. Well I couldn't see any markings on his car so I told Sophie to keep going. And he'd do that again, a second time. Viscously motioned for us to pull over. Then he'd get behind us. The third time he pulled up, at the same time there was someone trying to pass but couldn't because of this guy's maneuvers. The guy had a yellow roadster. He was a well-to-do young buck. And what he did was just put his bumper up against the other car (I think he was a angel) and he just shoved him over the hill and away they went 90 miles an hour. So I made the first right hand turn I could and got the heck out of there, but he sure was an angel to us. I don't know where he came from but he sure was welcome.

When I finished the 6 week course school, they hired me at Hay's Manufacturing Company as a riveter on wings. All of us were kind of cubby at first but we caught on. We were building booster bomber wings. They would fold up so they could park more planes on a carrier. That gave me a good income, enough that I could offer something. So I was able to marry, then rent a house and get some furnishings. I remember we got a little heater. This was Michigan winter. We had an upstairs apartment. We just about froze with that thing. I had to go to Sears to get an oil burner. A big one. We installed that and we were cozy. The guy living below us, I think he was renting also, he had the first floor and we had the second floor up. He and his wife Ester and they had a couple of kids. He went with me to riveting school. They made him a foreman right a way. And so I was in his department which worked out pretty good. We were putting up a lot of good wings.

But this time I remember, it was Spring, and he bought a box full of little chicks. Little yellow chicks. I don't know if it was his wife's birthday or what. Anyway he presented them to her. She thought that was the loveliest thing, these little chicks. She fixed up a place in the corner of the room. She put a light bulb in there for more heat and a feeder. She was enjoying them so much so he bought another box of them and not being a farmer he didn't realize how fast they would grow. He sort of lost interest in them right a way but her and the kids were enjoying them but man, in a couple, three weeks them things started roosting. They would roost on the back of the couch, back of the chairs. They were all over the house. And she threatened to divorce him if he didn't get them out of there.

So with Sophie working and me working, she was paying the bills and I was able to save up the money that I made. We were able to make a down payment on a little house. It was about two aches of ground near a golf course. And range experimental station in between. It was a shell of a house. It wasn't plastered inside yet and no electricity or water to it. But it was a house and that much land, for what they charged me was a bargain. I recognized it so we got it. But we didn't get a chance to live in it.

From 4F to A1 Overnight

I got drafted in spite of being a riveter and a married man, it didn't make any difference. They said my heart was enlarged and they didn't want me so they marked me 4F. So I kept on a working and then Franklin Delano Roosevelt, he was the president at that time, proclaimed that as of today all 4Fs will be 1As. And so I became 1A overnight and this time they presented me with a draft again. So Sophie saw me to the train. I kissed her goodbye and we loaded up and headed for Camp Custer. I expected that I'd be on the front lines any day now but we landed in Camp Custer and they trotted us all out. They separated us out, the fat ones from the skinny ones and they started calisthenics for the fat ones. And then they asked, "Who volunteered and who was drafted?" They then separated us again. All those that volunteered to one side all those drafted to the other side. We all did this and then they made an announcement, they said, "All those that were drafted can go home for three weeks to settle your affairs. And now you are getting a check from the army every month. We pay your food and everything else." They gave us our clothes, mostly fatigues, working cloths. And then they said, "All the others that volunteered are going for training now for the army."

So that's how it happened. Those that volunteered really volunteered. They put them to work right a way, basic training in the hills somewhere. I don't know where. But the rest of us went home for three weeks. That was a regular vacation. I didn't have to work. Sophie and I would go to Little Pine Island and swim and boat around. We use to rent a boat and paddle out to the island and have our picnics.

Tape 4, SideA

Basic Training

They gave us some rags and bammies and put us to work washing windows. What is this anyway? Getting good young vigorous people and getting them to washing windows. But that was only for a little while. For basic training they shipped us off to Arkansas. There I got to meet Lieutenant Ray. He was assigned to us. There we formed into platoons. He took us out on a hill to evaluate us for cadre. They desperately needed leaders to handle all these people coming in. So they were trying to select the best boys that could be trained to become corporals and eventually sergeants and eventually take over the leadership. So this lieutenant Ray was a nice looking guy; big man. He had a crew haircut and he was one of the most agile men I had ever seen. One of the trainings was he would fire orders at us and we were to execute them as fast and as many as we could. He would select the people he wanted for cadre. I heard him say, "Forward march". So I started marching along briskly and I didn't hear him say, "To the rear march," which mean you abruptly turn around and come back. That part I didn't hear. I heard some one following me, so I kept right on a'goen. I kind of wondered where the heck I was go'en. But I didn't hear any other orders. I found myself at the bottom of a big hill there in Arkansas. All of a sudden I heard someone yell'en and I looked up and there was a whole bunch of guys and the officer standing there watching us two guys. So they gave us the signal to "double-time" us to come back. We had to run all the way up the hill back again. So that cooked my goose as far as being a leader of any kind.

This camp was known as Camp Robinson. We were training a-way and one of the devices they had there was walking or jumping over the wall. This wall was about eight foot high. They would train you to run and put your foot against it and walk the first two steps right up the wall and volt the rest of the way. We would catch our fingers on top of it and volt over it. Very few people could do it. I couldn't do it but this lieutenant Ray could do it with ease. He would run up to it and walk up two or three steps and then he would jump over it. But like I said he was very exceptional.

Once in a while we would take a walk of 20 miles with full field packs just to check our stamina, which wasn't very good. We'd start marching with these packs and there'd be a truck following us to pick up the guys with too bad of blisters on their feet. The General would park his jeep at the crossroad, to see what condition we were in.

We had two pairs of shoes a piece. I'd take one size too small and another regular. I'd break in the small pair so they would just fit my feet. I'd use them for the hikes. So my foot wouldn't be moving in my shoe using every ounce of strength would go into walking. It worked out good. I never got any blisters. Lieutenant Ray would walk to the front of the line. We were walking two by two and then he would turn around and walk all the way back, checking the men, seeing how they were doing. I noticed once in a while he would be caring two packs. He would take someone else's field pack and help him out so he could keep up better. He would notice the person who was lagging. He would take his pack and carry it for him. He was a regular man. He was a great man. I wouldn't mind going to war with someone like that.

So I noticed when night come we were still marching or walking rather, hiking two by two. There was a jeep parked there at the crossroads with its lights shining on the men as they walked by the light of the jeep. And those were the generals that were in the jeep and they were checking the men over to see what condition they were in. It must have been close to the end of the 20 miles. The lieutenant kept nagging us. He said, "When you walk by that Jeep, straighten up. Straighten up and walk briskly." It made him look like a good officer to train men to be able to hike 20 miles and still be able to walk briskly and upright.

At the end of our training there, the Generals would come over. They sat on a platform to view the soldiers. We had to put on our class A uniforms and line up in the hot Arkansas sun. The place that we were training looked like a desert. We were lined up waiting for the generals to get there. Of course we were there an hour a head of time or maybe two hours. I know some of the guys would pass out in the heat. But finally they come and mounted that platform and we had to march briskly before them, give them the right hand salute. And all it was military to meet the band.

And then the General was very pleased and he announced on the speaker that half of us were to remove our shirts and the others to keep their shirts on and we were to form two football teams and play one against the other. He was going to watch it all from the platform. Well, maybe it was because I was a farm boy but I didn't like to ware so many cloths so didn't ware my undershirt. The officer kept yelling at me, "Take off your shirt! Take off your shirt!" So I took it off. When he saw I didn't have an undershirt on he started yelling, "Put your shirt back on! Put it on!" But it was too late and the General saw me in my bare skin and I heard him hollering, "Send that man to me. Send him to me." Man, I slowly walked across the whole parade ground; gave him a solute all the while feeling like a naked chicken there…a plucked chicken there in front of him. He said, "See that canyon over there? (There was a big canyon over there) Fill it up with rocks." So everyone was playing football and I was filling it with rocks. I was so glad when he finally went away.

I Came to Cook

Then they were going to take us to a bivouac. A bivouac is a camping in the woods under battle field conditions. We went out there and it was like a jungle. I never saw anything like it. There were briers and something that looked like barbed wire strung through the briers. You couldn't walk through those woods. It was impossible. You had to hack your way through with a machete. In this area where we were, they set up their kitchen and there was a lake nearby. You had to go around about five miles to get to the lake with a Jeep to get the water. We started hacking a path through because the lake wasn't very far from where we were camping but to get to it was difficult. So when one group was called to training the other group would start hacking away with machetes. We didn't really have machetes, we had bayonets and they weren't very sharp either. Finally we hacked a path through it. Awww, that water was delightful. It was sun heated warm water so we spent a lot of time swimming there, every chance we would get.

This one time I was helping in the kitchen and I didn't get my tent set up yet. It was two half shelter haves. Usually you buddied up with someone. He would have half the shelter-half and the other person would have the other half and if you buckled them together it would form a tent. But I carried two of those so I wouldn't have t sleep with anyone. I got in late and began to look around for a good place to set up my tent and there were two logs laying parallel: ideal place for a tent. I didn't know why anyone hadn't taken that spot. Everyone was snoring by then. I set my tent up, pulled up some Spanish moss and put a couple arm full of that and spread it out, laid my blanket over it and it made a nice soft bed. I was pretty tired and went to sleep. Sometime during the night, I felt a weight on my chest. I was lying on my back and knew it was some kind of snake. But I didn't know if it was a poison snake or not, a rattler or what. I breathed kind of shallow and laid there hoping that daylight would come and I could see what it was. I was sweating in every pore. I guess it wore me out and I dozed off and went to sleep. When I woke up that thing was gone. I looked on the outside of the tent and there was the snake. It was a black snake, pretty good size, probably three or four feet long, maybe. Later on the guys told me to get my tent out of there because that was a rattle snake nest there and that's why no one put their tent there. Later on I found out that these black snakes are mortal enemies of the rattler and will kill the rattler where ever they see them. So this black snake was guarding me all through the night from being bitten from one of these rattlers.

Something like this happened to me before. This was back when I was working for Mr. Baker yet at the riding academy. Bud his boy and I would go along with a group of women who came riding there on Thursday. They would usually ride in the woods to an area that was close to a hamburger joint. They would all go in there to eat and Bud and I would have to take care of their horses. We would tie a rope from one tree to another and then we would snub these horses to this rope. This one time was a nice sunny day so we stretched out in the sun to take a little snooze while we had the opportunity. All of a sudden I saw Bud jump 10 feet from a laying position. I wondered what was going on. A snake was coming right at him. Apparently the snake was frightened by the horses stomping around and it was getting a way from the horses and didn't see us laying there. And Bud later on told me it was coming right at me. It looked like a blue racer. I didn't know. I was still laying there and the snake ran on top of me and made a U- turn and took off in the other direction. It all happened so fast that I didn't get a chance to even become frightened.

So anyway I moved my tent out of there. Later on someone caught that black snake, killed it and skinned it. But I was sorry to see it go. I didn't know it was protecting me, Otherwise I would have protected it too. Ever since then I look out for black snakes and I appreciate them. They kill all kinds of bugs and other bad snakes. I appreciate to have them around the camp.

We eventually finished our basic training and were all ready for the heavy stuff. I wanted to be signed up for the cavalry where they had horses. But they told me that they no longer used horses in the army. The cavalry now consisted of a half-track and a truck type thing and a Jeep and they would go out ahead of everyone and scout out where the enemy was. I wasn't particularly interested in anything like that. They knew I had cooked in the CC camp and they needed cooks so they put me in cooking school to brush up on cooking. It had been a while since I did it. And then they sent me to a kitchen to cook there was already two cooks there. I was the third man. One was an Indian and one was a Mexican, both excellent cooks. The Mexican owned his own restaurant at one time. This Indian was the first cook. He wouldn't just cook what was on the menu he could always make something extra. Like if he was boiling ham, he would save the stock and add tomatoes to it and some macaroni and make excellent soup out of it which wasn't on the menu at all. Many of those things he'd do. But I walked in there and they asked me what I was doing there. I said, "They sent me over here."

"What for? " They asked. "To cook" I said.

They set down at a table and said, "Alright then, go ahead and cook." And they wouldn't move. So I looked at the menu as it was and it had spaghetti and cheese with tomatoes sauce. That is something I like very well and cooked many times over. So I whacked up a bunch of cheese and cooked my macaroni and got the thing go'en. When it came out excellent they said, "Yeah, you're a cook." And they accepted me then.

Then each afternoon when my shift was finished, when we had gotten dinner fixed and served it, then we could go home and stay overnight and come back next morning. We'd take over the kitchen and do dinner again. It worked out nice. The meat would come in the halves of a cow or a quarter and a whole lamb would come and we would have to cut it up. The pork would come the same way, in halves. So it would take us a while to get everything cut up the night before for the next day but also it would give us an opportunity to snip out the tenderloin from the beef. The officers often wondered, "What happened to the tenderloin? We never get any tenderloin." Well we cooks ate it. Some of it I would cut up into a butterfly slices and I would pack it into my overnight bag when I would be going home. Sometimes I would slip a ham in there if it was a nice little ham. So it provided Sophie with some good meat. Once in a while the people she was staying with would be questioning her. "Where'd you buy that?" She'd say, "aww, a little store down the line." They could never find the little store down the line. These were good places to work. There were only 200 men in the company. We would be responsible for the food for those 200 only.

Moved to Tyler, Texas

But now the camp moved to Tyler, Texas and at that place was a sixteen hundred man-mess. There the dining room was like a wagon wheel where several dining rooms circled the hub of the kitchen. The kettles in the kitchen were steam kettles and were about six feet across and were three feet deep and that's what we were to cook in. We couldn't provide really a decent meal. We provided food like stew or curry rice, things like that. The darn weevils would get into the rice and would come to the top of the kittle. We would have to keep mixing them in. But it looked alright after it was cooked.

I had a second cook. He was a little Chinese guy, a very clever fellow. He told me once that he was sent over to United States to study American army ways and then report back to China.

He says, "When we are fighting you then we will know all about you but you won't know anything about us." I said Lee, "Listen, America and China are friends. They are not going to ever going to fight."

"Yah, but we will know all about you but you won't know anything about us."

He was very clever. We had to break eggs, cases and cases of eggs for breakfast. And we'd all sit around in a circle and break these eggs into a kettle and then we had a 50 gallon garbage can in the middle. A regular metal oil drum with the top cut out. After a while it would be full of egg shells. Lee was agile and he would jump in there and tramp them down. We would be laughing and kidding him when he was in there but when his back was turned instead of breaking the eggs, we would just throw the egg and all in there as he was dancing by. He didn't know what was happening until the eggs started running into his shoes. Then he found out he was all splattered with the eggs on the back. Kind of cruel but at that time it seemed to be alright, at least for us because we had a laugh out of it. Poor little Lee had to go change cloths and dump the eggs out of his shoes. I remember one time he and I were hitch-hiking to Taylor, Texas and there was an officer driving by and Lee was running. I don't know what he was running for but he would solute the lieutenant while running. The officer stopped and told us that it is not military. "Don't run and salute." Anyway he gave us a ride and asked us how we were doing in our kitchen. Lee let his hair down. He says, "They don't ever give us enough eggs and we have to add milk to the eggs to scramble them and make them go around. It used to be that we would eat eggs ourselves but not anymore."

That guy said, "I'm the mess officer for this outfit. I'll see if I could get more eggs."

He got told off by Lee and we use to eat eggs before but no longer because we have to put milk in them.

While we were in Arkansas, Sophie was with child and she was staying in a place with a couple old maids and they were looking forward to taking care of the newborn. So we would go to see the army camp doctor. He was a young lieutenant. He was very capable and very embarrassed at the same time because he was use to treating boys not a woman. But he did a good job of examining her and measuring her and all that goes with it. He kept a watch on her weight.

Sophie's Brother Killed

As it happened Sophie's brother, Stanley, was in an airplane accident. The army airplane was flying from Grand Rapids to California and he caught a ride on it. It didn't clear the mountains.

The down draft dragged it down and smashed into the side of the mountain and killed everybody. As it happened, Stanley had been writing a letter to Sophie and he had it addressed to her. So when they found the letter, they knew Sophie was a relative. So the MPs came over to see her. They explained what happened. They found out the home address. So we checked with headquarters and got a pass to go home back to Grand Rapids, Michigan to console her mother. We did this. Sophie stayed then for the delivery in her home town. I went back to Taylor to go back to work again.

Eventually when the baby was so old, she wanted to come over. I tried to locate a place for her to stay. I checked the town out. It was a nice town. It had a square in the middle like a park. There were no cars there. You could walk around on the outside. It was a country of roses. They raised roses there. Not for the flower but for the shrub. So it was always pretty with an abundance of flowers around there. But anyway, I tried to get us a place to stay but the man said that it would cost forty dollars a month. Forty dollars was all the money that we got for Sophie to live on per month. I didn't know what to do. He said, "Everyone gets rich during the war and I never got rich during the last war but that's not what's going to happen now. Now I'm going to be in the money." But I didn't rent his forty dollar room. I took off hitch-hiking back to camp pretty disgusted.

Sophie and Baby Frances

A guy picked me up and he had a Pontiac coup, just like the one I use to drive. His name was Franklin. He was an old farmer. I told him about this guy wanting to charge me forty dollars, all my money. He was intending to get rich from this war. He got so mad he said, "If I had a grenade I would roll it under his door. You come and live with me" he said. So we went over to look at his place. He had a nice little house. He just got married to a 70 year old school teacher. Her name was Nan. They had several cows and a barn and a nice team of mules and a dug well like you would see in a pretty picture book. It was a well with rocks around it and a little roof and a crank and a rope. You let the bucket down and crank the bucket up like you did 100 years ago.

But that was the best water, cold and clear. His house was up on a sand hill, I don't know how the water got up there.

But when Sophie came, they welcomed her like their own daughter. They couldn't do enough for little Franny. Nan would want to baby sit so bad. She would try to get us out of the house, so she would tell Franklin, "Let them have the car, let them have the car. They have to see the countryside." So they would send us off with his car to cruse around through this beautiful landscape of roses and they would play with the baby. Come evening, they had two swings facing one another. Sophie and I would sit on one and Nan and Frank would sit on the other one and we would talk but we couldn't quite match our talk. I would tell them about the draft horses we used on our farm and wondered why he didn't have horses. And he said that horses aren't as good. Mules are better. Their temperament is much better. I said "Na, horses are much better."

So then we'd go on about something or another and then eventually I found out he didn't know about the draft horses, the heavy ones. The draft horses were very docile. But he was thinking of broncos, the wild horses that they had running around out there on the prairie. That was his concept of horses. So no wonder he was using mules. Well, this one day he was saying that he needed to bring his stove in because winter was coming. I said, why don't you leave it till next day and I will help you bring it in. I was thinking it was one of those upright cast iron stoves like we had in Michigan, coal burners. "No, no." He said. "I can carry it with one hand." What the heck kind of stove was that? It turned out to be a little tin stove that had one burner on top. He said, "My problem will be getting wood." I asked, "How many cords will you need to run through winter?" He said, "About half a cord." I said, "What?!" "Yup" he said. "If it is a bad winter it will take about a half a cord." I said, "Holy mackerel! Where's your ax?"

So he gave me an ax and Sophie and I went out to a pot hole that was his woods. There was elder there. The elders were at the most two inches across and they were quite tall. There was a stump there. I cut one of the elders and Sophie would hold it over the stump and I would then cut it into stove size chunks. We worked there about a short half day. We had about half a cord cut up for him. I told him your wood is cut up there. He said," well I'll hitch my mules tomorrow to the wagon and I'll go get it."

When I would go over there, I would carry my overnight bag and I would still furnish them with some of the best meat you could get during the war. And he would keep asking Sophie, "Where do you get such good meat?" She was now eating with them and she use to have her own little kitchen but they kept her for company. They wanted her for company so they made a few more biscuits. Their breakfast would be biscuits and jam. They would have several different kinds of jam. So Franklin would put one type of jam on one biscuits and a different kind of jam for another biscuits and that's how he made his breakfast. Those biscuits were delicious! And they were good cooks in them there days.

Moved to Tyler, Texas

Well, so again, the camp was getting ready to move to Florida this time we packed everything. The stoves had to be packed on the freight. Everything we had, the whole camp. All the equipment was going with us so they wired everything down and were busy as beavers, the whole camp. We hated to leave Franklins because it was a great place to stay and we had become such great friends and we will never forget them people. Again I don't think I was very honest with the army and they weren't very honest with me either. I told them that I could drive to Florida. They said, "If you have a car then come over and we'll give you tickets for gasoline and also money for food. You'll need food to get there. And so we will give you 5 days to get there. That ought to be enough." So they provided me with all this stuff and then the whole caboodle got on the train and took off. So I went over to get Sophie. We said farewell to Franklins and she had fried up a chicken for us. Southern style and put it in a shoe box for our lunch. We went to the bus station and got a ticket on the bus and we had goofed around a day or so already but we started out on this bus for Florida. It was nice riding. People were friendly in there. They fussed with the baby. They were all interested in the kid. So the first morning we woke up in that bus and we were in Florida already. And it was kind of dark and it was the first time we saw Spanish moss. It looked so spooky to us as we went through the foggy country with the moss hang'en from the trees. Pretty soon the bus went poop-poop-shrug and it stopped. And everybody was frustrated except Sophie the baby and myself. We took a blanket and spread it out on a nice grassy place along side the road and made ourselves comfortable and opened up that shoe box and man, it was full of solid fried chicken. Makes my mouth water just to think about it. There we were chomm'en on the fried chicken like a bunch of kings and everybody looken at us thought the window of the bus. They eventually fixed it somehow and we got to Stark, Florida. It was little more time until we pulled into the bus station. Then we got a hold of a taxi cab driver and asked him where we could find a place to rent a room. Well that is a mighty scarce commodity with a bunch of soldiers around and all their wives all look'en for the same thing. So we drove. This bus driver drove us all over the place. But there was nothing available. So I think Sophie stayed overnight with the driver and his wife. He took her home with him and then the next day when I came up there he showed us a cabin out in the cow pasture.

Tape 4, Side B

Song…*Strawberry Roan*

Camp Moves to Florida

The next day when I come back to town, I had located a place and Sophie had located a place. Mine looked like a better place, a one room in a two story house. And every room had an occupant, even the porch. It had paper around it and a girl was living in there. Another one was living in the garage. So it was that crowded. Of course there was only one toilet and that was on the back porch too. It was difficult; in fact, I was very embarrassed at one time. While we were living there a roomer went around that there was a window peeper and that somebody would be looking in the window at night. Well, there was one time I had to go make a nature call so I went across the road.

There was a woods back there and it looked like it was a fairly safe place. I started doing "my thing" and somebody noticed me walking around there outside because they called the whole caboodle out. They all came outside the house with flashlights and they started looking for this guy, the window peeper.

There I was, my pants were down and I couldn't do nothing and they kept coming closer and closer to me. I couldn't sit still any longer because the very next moment all their flashlights would be shining on me. So I grabbed my pants in my hands and I was going to head deeper into the woods and there was a tamarack tree laying there and I ran right into this tamarack tree. And when its dry it has claws sticking out all over that grabs you and there I was in the middle of that thing fighting the bushes trying to get through the darn tree branches and there they come with the flashlights, chasing. But I managed somehow in desperation to rip through and get myself together and took off down the road. Eventually I lost them all. When I came back they were still standing around there and they asked, "Did you get him?" I said, "no, but I chased him as far as I could go but I could not catch up with him, the dirty son-of-a-gun." But it was me all along trying to get away from them.

Well if we got up early enough in the morning, we could have pecans. If we didn't the pigs would beat us to it. But it was a nice place. We would spread a blanket out in the sun and we would all be sunbathing. All the women would come out and sun bath with us. Sophie wanted some place to leave baby Fran when she would be doing washing and stuff. So I bought some chicken wire and made a pen. We put all her playthings in there and a blanket and we tried to get her interested in staying in this pen but ohhh no, she wouldn't do it. She'd throw everything back out and want to crawl out of that thing. So I put a rubber band one of her favorite dolls that she kept throwing out. Then when she threw it out, it would spring back in again. That would make her fierce. So I figured, I would go and lay down in that pen and maybe she would want to come in and lay down with me. So there I was lying in the pen and she was on the outside, having a ball. She didn't fall for that one bit.

One day I was walking through the woods there and there were blackberries, everywhere I looked big ones, heavy ones. So when I got home I told Sophie about them and she said, "Let's go get um." She says, "I have beans cooking on the stove." I said, "Why don't we just turn the fire real low and then maybe when we come back we can have dinner." It takes a long time to cook beans. So we did that, turned the fire real low, took the kid. We had a perambulator then. We went out picking these blackberries. We got so involved picking the berries we forgot about the last thing we thought of which was the beans cooking on the stove, yah know. And when we got back there was smoke coming from the windows and smoke coming from under the door. All the people were ready to break the door down. They were hollering at us. Not only was the beans burnt but the kettle was burnt also so we couldn't use the kettle anymore and for a cook this was very embarrassing.

Another night I went to that lavatory on the back porch. The door wasn't locket so I opened it up and there was a women sitting there. Being a gentleman I tried to apologize, "I'm sorry" I said, "I didn't realize…" she said, "Get out of here! Close the door! Just get out!" She didn't even accept my apology!

The war went on. It didn't want to stop. They gave me an assignment to cook on a troop train. You know, a train that carries troops. They were hauling these boys to Baltimore and shipping from Baltimore to wherever they were going. I imagine to Europe was where they went from Baltimore. So we had a cook-car where we had stoves that were wired down to the floor. They were gas fire stoves. They were not very big but had a nice grill on top where we could fry eggs to order. Whatever they wanted. Two hundred men weren't hard to cook for. We could give them what kind of eggs they wanted…sunny side up or well done or light over, whatever they preferred and we have homemade bread and whatever else we cooked. I don't even remember now anymore. When we would unload the troops in Baltimore then they would give us a first-class ticket to come back to Florida. That first-class ticket had quite a bit of difference between that and the second-class ticket. So we would turn them in for the cash and would then always have a pocket full of money to come home with. That went on for quiet some time. One day I wanted to ride first class to see what it was like. So I got on the first-class car and I never had such luxury. I was the only one in the car. It was just like sitting in the living room in the softest chair you had. There was no noise there. You couldn't hear the rails but only a little sizzle from the air-conditioning. There were rugs all around. It was really luxurious riding in those days.

Nobody Gets a Pass

Well, it was getting time for our company to start packing up but first we were going to have one little bivouac again so we all went out to the woods and set up our tents. The officers had a big tent. They set it up for themselves. They put guards on the little dirt road running in there. You had to have a pass word before they allowed anyone to come in. So these officers, it was a first Lieutenant, he was in charge of the whole ca-bang. Also 3 or 4 other lieutenants, maybe 5. They got themselves some cases of beer and they were going to relax, (which they well deserved after training us for 6 weeks.) Apparently when they bought the beer someone turned them in to the higher authorities because they no sooner began to relax with this beer and here comes the commanding officer, the General of the whole thing. He has a red flag on his Jeep and a wild sort of driver. Here they come and the guards trying to stop them but they would pay no attention to these guards. They just burrowed right up to this officer-tent. The General walked in on them. And I don't know what he said. Apparently he threatened to send them out to the Russian front because I'd never seen such scarred commanding officers. After the General left, the lieutenants were so scarred of doing something wrong.

So when they told us we would be going overseas, my wife and baby were still there so I wanted to take them back home and get them situated. But he said, "Nobody gets passes. Absolutely, no reason, nobody gets passes." But as it happened, while I was cooking the back door opened and a captain walked in. He was a stranger, I hadn't seen him before. So I hollered, "attention" and my whole crew stood at attention and he come over and he said, "I have to work in the office and this time of day I would like some coffee so I thought I would come over to your kitchen to see if you could get me some coffee. Don't call "attention" next time I come," he said. So I said, "Fine". I provided some coffee for him and whatever I had, cake, donuts sometimes. Sometimes I would even sit down and talk with him a while. And this day I was telling him my problem, I said, "my wife, my daughter, little baby are here. I had nothing arranged for them and now they tell me I have to go overseas. I don't know how the heck long I am going to be there." I said, "It's a way in Michigan." He said, "Well, if a baby is sick, they got to give you a pass." I said, "She's sick." Well that wasn't all together wrong. She had an ear ache infections quite frequently and she'd really cry. It would really hurt her. We didn't know what it was that was hurting her. So he said, "Ok, I'll make out a pass."

So I went back home to where Sophie stayed. I figured there was no use working anymore. They were all shipping out. So I hung around for a couple-three days then I figured I better go see what's going on or I'll be AWOL of something. I met our top sergeant at the bus stop. I said, "Did I get a pass yet?" He said, "Nobody gets a pass." I said to myself, "Oh no, something's wrong here." So I get back to camp and get on a bicycle and paddle over to this captain's office and I'm telling him that everyone's moving out and I didn't get that pass yet. "Well, just go back to camp," he says. "I'll get it for you." But before I could get back to camp I heard them hollering, "Novak, report to headquarters. Novak, headquarters!" So I went over there and this first Lieutenant, the commanding officer, was standing there with the pass in his hand with a very baffled look on his face. "Here's a pass for you, but I didn't have nothing to do with it. I want you to know that I had nothing to do with it." "I know" I said. "I know you didn't." I was going to say more but I didn't want to embarrass him anymore. He was sure puzzled.

England

So Sophie and I want home and everyone else went to fight the war. Eventually I was told to report to Baltimore. But when I got there the ship hadn't come in yet. So they told me to go sightseeing or something. So I spent several days goofing around, Washington DC and that area around Baltimore. There wasn't much too see in Baltimore but Washington was nice. Eventually the ship came. It was Wakefield. It was a luxury ship really. It ordinarily would hold five thousand passengers. I think it held quite a bit more when it came to solders. And each of us was loaded down with equipment. We had a regular pack and a duffle bag and a mask and a double helmet and then a horseshoe pack on top of the whole thing. It weighed about seventy pounds. The barracks bag full of blankets and stuff. What they were doing was using us as an insurance that the equipment would get to Europe. And if any of it got lost then we were responsible for it.

So we were insuring it that it would get across for them. They were pretty smart. The stuff wasn't for us. We couldn't use all the stuff that we carried. But this ship was a fast one but they didn't have any escort for it because it was supposed to be able to outrun the subs. The German subs were hanging around Baltimore because they knew darn well that we embarked from Baltimore. And there was an iron fence under the water where ships couldn't get through and the gate had to be opened to get out of there. So the submarines couldn't get in there. And just as the first ship went out, it was immediately torpedoed. And the boys didn't even have a drill to know what to do in case of being torpedoed. Some would be climbing down into the water and others would be coming up because the water was too cold. And it was a mess. We lost lot of men for nothing. But anyway we got out safely into the ocean. But there were many times that, "man your battle stations" would be called. And we would sweat it out until the, "all clear" would be sounded.

We had 2 meals a day and the ship would rock and that time of year and the food would be spilt all over the floor. I couldn't eat in there. The 2 meals, I couldn't eat either one of them. So I'd grab me an apple or an orange and that's what I lived on. Eventually we landed in England. There we came lugg'en the equipment, the barracks bag and everything else. The British solders were small, like "Little People" but they were very agile. They come charging up the gang plank and they'd grab our bags, grab our equipment and they'd carry it for us. We'd go down the plank and the British WACS were there with a big kettle. And coffee that looked like mother would make with cream and sugar mixed in. It would be handy that way. We had these cups that held almost a quart, and these girls would fill it right up full. Good hot stuff. And I tried to drink it and it was green tea! British drink. They hadn't had coffee since nobody knows when. But they preferred tea anyway. It was their drink. So I had to get use to it.

Eventually there was this beer they had and it comes in big barrels. They called it, "bitters." It was kind of bitter but it wasn't too bad. It was dark beer, similar to our Bach Beer that we have over here. And these barrels would have 2 wagon wheels. They had tunnels there and they would back the barrels into this tunnel. They'd have a plank for a bar and they would already have a beer garden. They had it all set up and all you needed is money. They could furnish you with beer.

I was amazed at the country. The chateaus were off in the distance. We never even got close to them. There was a lot of land there that looked like sheep pasture because the grass was pastured down like a golf course. And the trees! I never saw such beautiful trees. Huge! They were monsters. A whole company could sit under one of these trees and they would all be in the shade. We would hold our meetings under these big trees. The country side had little narrow roads and had roses growing on either side. Looked like wild roses, I don't know. There would be a valley and there would be a little stream running through it. There would be fishermen there fishing from this little stream. There'd be a cottage with a thick yellow roof. It looked like it was made out of straw. It would look just like a picture book. I asked these soldiers, I asked, "why are you helping us like that?" They said, "Well, you come here to help us."

We were always changing money so we changed our American money for British money. They had pounds and sixpence and three pence. Their pound was worth 4 dollars. So we were on top of that. We'd be gambling, our soldiers would be using a pound as a dollar bill but that thing was worth $4.00.

England is Overloaded, Shove Off

We didn't stay very long in England. England was overloaded with people and equipment and stuff. They had to move us out as soon as they could so we got on this ship and headed out for ETO, European Theater of Operation, headed for Omaha

Beach. The boys had already landed and secured this beach a few days earlier. But as we were coming close I was amazed to see the ships, the graveyard of ships, as far as you could see were sunk up to as far as 5 or 6 feet. Somebody had told me this was done on purpose to form a water break so other ships could enter into this collmer of water. So they brought a little boat, one of those iron contraptions and we were all moved into that. It took us right to the shore line. We didn't even have to get our feet wet.

Next thing that amazed me was these balloons. The sky was covered with them with cables anchoring them down. Apparently that was to keep the German Luftwaffe from getting down too close to the solders down there for strafing. So if they stayed above the balloons then our gunners could reach them with our anti aircraft guns. Anyway they had that all anchored down when we got there. Well then there was this long line of men marching up this sand mountain, hill, single file, just like ants and I was soon one of them. It was difficult. I had a heavy pack to carry. I don't know what it was, I guess I wasn't as physically well as the rest of them because they would get ahead of me but I would keep right on a-comm'en. After we finally got to the top and it flattened out, the boys would drop down to rest and I would catch up to them. And that was a signal to them that when I got there everybody was to jump up and start hiking again. So I never got a chance to sit down or lay down to get a breath. But I kept on a-slugg'en.

Never Stayed Long Anywhere

There were these graveyards, and everywhere you could see, it looked like acres of white crosses. Our men that soldiered there were already buried. We were following on the heals of the attacking soldiers. And we would be replacements for the fallen troops up ahead. We finally come to a little town, and on the edge of town was an old shack there. I don't know what it was but it had a manger in it, one manger. Quite a good size structure, all beat up. So a bunch of us moved into that thing for the night. I cleaned out the manger and it made a real good bed. Some of the boys were preparing a stove as it was getting pretty cold at night. I went into town to see if I could find some sort of light. There was some sort of French store and they had a lamp but it didn't have a chimney on it but it had some kerosene yet. So I bought it and was caring it, going back to this barn and people were laughing at me while I walked along with this lantern. They were talking to me too but I didn't get the gist of it. As it turns out, at one time there was a philosophizer walking around with a lamp looking for the Just-Man. And that was what they were referring to me.

But anyway I got back to the shack there and there was a Red Cross tent near by. I picked up a Zane Gray book. It was a novel. I found a fruit jar and made me a chimney out of it. So there I had this bunk and I had a light and by that time a fire was going and it was nice and warm in there. I was reading, relaxing. A Lieutenant walked in. He was checking up on the boys. He was amazed at how cozy we had made ourselves for the night. We never knew how long we were going to stay anywhere. We never stayed long anywhere. He said that there was a group of boys who came to his tent and said, "Nobody issued us beds to sleep on yet." They were waiting for them to issue beds so they could go to sleep for the night. He was amazed at how dumb they could be after all the training they received. He was also amazed at how comfy we could make ourselves.

Going through this town, I was surprised to see that they had urinals right off the sidewalks. Against the building-wall and men would just turn their back to the people walking by and do-their-thing. On the corners of the street there would be toilets. It was just an enclosure and you could see the feet of the person who was using this facility whether it was a man or a woman in there. They didn't have any stools like we have. They had a ceramic plate with 2 foot steps that were sunk in a little bit so you wouldn't slide and a ceramic hole. And that's what they would use. They were not inhibited like we are. They were very open people. That's what amazed me.

There was one time we found a river. We were all sweaty and dirty so the boys just stripped and jumped into this river. And I don't know if it was Sunday or what day it was but these citizens, a girl and a man would be walking along, arm-in-arm, and visiting with these bare naked soldiers. They would be asking if we could spare a little soap because they hadn't any soap for a long time. It was a very scarce commodity for them.

This part of the country we were in was called Normandy. It was unique in that it had the fields enclosed in hedgerows. They called them hedgerows which are ancient rock walls. They had been overgrown in many, many centuries with brush and small trees. They formed walls. Our tanks and men had an awful time getting through this mess because no one had foreseen this thing. All the intelligence had never foreseen this situation. The Germans could shoot from the back of these hedgerows. Well this one time, there was kind of a low spot in one of these hedgerows; they were usually 5-6 foot high or maybe even higher. There was an opening and everyone dropped down on their hands and knees and was crawling along past this area. We had one guy by the name of Johnny, he was a comic all the time, so when everyone was crawling he took a clod of dirt and threw it at the fellow in front of him and it hit him on the back. Well, the fellow got scarred and began to holler, "I'm hit, I'm hit! Medic, Medic!" And Johnny couldn't help it, he started laughing. The Germans were mad because we were laughing.

Paris Hadn't Been Liberated Yet

At this time Paris hadn't been liberated yet and there was a lot of fighting going on. The thing was, we were sticky and dirty and I was afraid I'd get bugs in my cloths. So when we had a chance to stop and camp for a few days, I got a hold of a tin can about 5 gallons. I got some water from this muddy stream, the best I could and then I started a fire. I got this water to boiling and then I stuck my jacket in it. I thought it would kill the bugs. One of the corners of my jacket slipped out of the pot without my noticing it and it burned. Burned off one of the corners of my jacket. So all the time I was there in Europe I was walking around with one corner of my jacket burned off. You're not getting any new cloths.

When we finally got to Paris there was a WMCA building. It had an Olympic size swimming pool in it and it wasn't destroyed. So we were able to get cleaned up and go swimming in that thing. We were camping not too far away and I'd slip over there every chance I'd get and swim in that pool. It was so delightful during the middle of the war. We were constantly on the tail of them that were really doing the fighting.

This one time we had been out in the country for maybe a week trailing along following the troops and there was nothing much left in the towns or other parts of the country after the battles. So our company stopped for the night and somebody told me that there was a little town and at the other end of it was a shower. It was cold out. We had everything on that we possessed, overcoat on top of everything else, big woolen ones that came down to your ankles. So I took a towel, I don't know where I got it, maybe it was a rag of some kind, and I started out for that shower. And I walked and walked. It must have been miles. I finally found it. I went in there and they had hot water! I just soaked and soaked. And then I got out and I didn't need the overcoat or my jacket. I had it all, the wool shirt and undershirt and helmet and now I was carrying all this stuff under my arm because once I got warmed up, I stayed warm all the way back to camp. I was surprised.

Bing Crosby

The evenings they would come up with entertainment. There would be a rattley old movie machine. I don't know if they had to crank it by hand yet, probably did. They would set it up in a barn in a hay mow and then we would crawl into this hay mow and the screen would be across the barn floor on the other barn wall. This was because we didn't dare show any light during the night because Luftwaffe was active. And they would spot anything like that. So we would watch a movie. Sometimes they would use a truck with covering on it. They would cover the back side with a sheet and then they would put a movie machine inside of this truck and the movie would come out real good on the outside. You couldn't tell whether the machine was on the outside or inside of the truck. It didn't make any difference. So we would watch a movie that way. We would be standing around watching that thing.

One time it happened. We were camping and were ordered to pick up our helmet and "March!" They marched us. We were pretty close to the front lines because the guns would be rattling the ground. Then we were seated on the side of a hill. There were more and more people coming, maybe a 1,000 soldiers all sitting on their helmets. It was typical to sit on our helmets because the ground was wet. We would sit on the steel part. We also had a plastic type liner and a sack type thing. So usually I would carry an extra pair of socks in there yet. I kept them in my helmet. I could wash them and they would dry. I always had clean dry socks (if I could find clean water). We were sitting on the hill and there was a little wooden stage at the bottom of the hill. And who do you think came out but Bing Crosby. He had a woman and a man with them and they put on a skit; she sold him a coat in a bag. He didn't see it until he bought it and then when he looked at it, he found it was so moth eaten that it wouldn't stick together. Anyway then he would sing. The trouble was that the electricity blew out so he had no electricity but he had a good voice and it would carry. He'd ask if anyone had a favorite song. Of course "White Christmas" was the favorite one at that time. So he would sing it.

Tape 5, Side A

Chinese Spy

was telling about living in an eight-man tent, of course we were sleeping on the ground and using cardboard or whatever we could find. A little stove was in the middle but we couldn't burn with it because there was no chimney to it. So I went over to the kitchen and they had tomato cans, the big ones. They were just about the right size. By cutting out the top and bottom and stacking them together it made an excellent chimney. We wired it up but then we didn't have any wood. Any tree that would be cut down, the Frenchmen would charge United States for it. So this one day an officer comes over, he knew the situation. He said, "Come on. We are all going for a little exercise. We'll go for a walk." He took us out into the woods where the woodcutters had been cutting wood. There was nobody there but there were stacks and stacks of wood. He said, "I'm going to be looking the other way and I don't care what you guys do." So we all grabbed a couple chunks of that wood and we marched back to camp with it. We sawed it up into small pieces, only about 6 to 8 inch pieces and then with our bayonets we were able to split it into fine wood and we would hide it under the sleeping bags. Once we got the fire going we would assign a guy to be up to stoke the fire. He'd be up for an hour and then he would wake another guy up and this guy would be up for a certain length of time until it would go all around the eight of us. We kept pretty cozy that way.

Well, Thanksgiving Day was coming around and one of the trucks went down to the docks. There was a ship there full of turkeys and they were dressed turkeys but they were not boxed or packaged in any way. So these guys loaded the turkeys on the truck like you would load cord wood, just as high as could stay on the truck. The turkeys were all around there bare naked, there wasn't any cover on them whatsoever. They brought them in and the cooks said, "We can't do anything with this stuff." And somebody said, "There's a bakery in Paris. Let's drive over there." So they drove to Paris and the baker cooked them for us. They had excellent baking facilities there. I don't know how many he cooked for us or how many he kept for himself, probably a small truck load. But that was alright because we all had some turkey to eat and they were eatable.

I run into the little Chinaman cook of mine, Lee. He had an idea that he didn't have to fight. He thought that if he got close to the front he could apply for officers mess and that they would accept him because he was a delicate little guy and very ambitious and they liked them kind for officers mess boys. And so that was his idea, anyway, he had a two shelter half like I had. One night we went out to a potato field to pick some potatoes. I never saw such big potatoes like that. It felt to me like there was a half bushel of potatoes under this one hill. I don't know how they did it but they sure did have good land and knew how to rotate the crops. Anyway, we got these potatoes and whacked them up and we didn't have any flour to make potato pancakes so we cooked them the best way we could. Who can eat that many potatoes?

This Lee would learn the languages. As we crossed the boarders from one country to the other they would issue us a little book of the translations of the languages from English to whatever country we were in, Belgium or wherever. He would learn it! He would take the little book into his tent and before you knew it he would be speaking French and we would take him along with us and he would order beer for us. He knew how to talk enough French or Belgium or wherever he was. I was curious about that and he said that he was chosen in China to be the one to join the American army as a spy because, he said, "We will know all about you but you won't know anything about us. I finally got him to teach me how to write my name in Chinese and it was up and down. But I learned to write it. When we got home, I went to a Chinese laundry that washed my shirts and when they wanted me to write my name I wrote it in Chinese. And they were so excited. They went up and got a chief and tried to quiz me but that's all I knew.

Wake Up, Something is Happening!

Near the German boarder the French, had numerous amount of caves in there. You'd look across the field and it would look like a bumpy cow pasture but it was all underground caves. As we were plodding along behind the troops, they would try to find us things to do. So they told us to get the sand that had sifted into these caves and clean them out. There was no end to them. I tried to walk through them but I didn't have a flash light and I didn't want to get too deep into them. As we were cleaning these we would run into people that had been buried in that sand. So we would just cover them up a little deeper and keep on a'going.

Well, we went into this Black Forest; I'm not sure what the name of it was. This time it was a Sergeant and he didn't have a partner so he came over with his shelter half the ones you buckle together to make a pup tent. So we decided to bunk together for the night. But it was such a quiet place and we had been digging these fox holes every night and staying only night in them so we decided not to dig one this night. I don't know what time it was, maybe 3 or 4 o'clock in the morning and really black in the forest and the sergeant started shaking me and he said, "You better wake up. Something is happening." And man was it ever happening! The Germans had some type of bombs that had wires on them that caused them to shriek when they were bombing or diving. It was to shake people up. And they were bombing something and it was shaking this forest. I didn't know that the trees could shake like that or that the earth could shake like that. But it was like being in a sifter. The trees were bending way down and them shrieking noises over our heads and this sergeant grabbed a'hold of his little shovel and he started digging. And it was a steady stream of dirt coming from his shovel just like out of a water hose. And I was sitting on my helmet trying to put my shoes on and I was laughing so much it was hurting my stomach just to watch him shovel. But I was scarred too so I joined him in that hole and we kept on a'digging and digging and finally got it up to our shoulders and then we dragged some logs over the top of it and then put dirt on top of that. By then it was morning and they yelled, "Load up." And we had to load up the trucks and we never even had a chance to sleep in our safe fox hole. Later on somebody said they had bombed and destroyed a bridge and that made it as tough as possible for reinforcements to move ahead.

Go and Smoke Them Out!

Next night or maybe a couple nights later we were again in a woods and this time I was digging and I dug into a pile of World War I armaments. All kinds of stuff: shells, bayonets and I don't know what it was. It must have been a junk pile or someplace where they buried the armaments. But there was nothing that I was interested in. Again, sometime during the night the sergeant woke me up and he said, "There are a group of enemy and they are firing on our trucks." As the convoy trucks would be going through the woods they would be hiding there and would blaze away at them and destroy them. Their high powered rifles would do a lot of damage. So we were told to go and smoke them out.

And black! So black you couldn't see your hand in front of your face. Apparently we were caring phosphate bombs or grenades or something that contained phosphate because they sprinkled this phosphate on the ground and made paths. You could follow these things and get around in the woods at that time of night. I guess they over ruled the Geneva Convention regarding phosphate shells. They had phosphate from something and it must have been shells. So they had this trail going to the armament tent, so we could load up on whatever ammunition we wanted, hand grenades or whatever. So I went over there and got a couple hand grenades and more ammunition and started down a trail with a bunch of guys. Well, we were taught never to bunch up but to space out. So I let them guys go ahead and I guess they were spacing themselves out down this dirt road toward where these Germans were suppose to be.

Every once in a while there would be a guard along the road and they had a pass word. They would say this word to the guard so he would know who was going by and wouldn't shoot. It seemed like these guys stopped about 50 feet from me, maybe. I was wondering what they were waiting for and finally I figured out that I better walk over there to see what's going on. I walked over there and there was a group of guys and they were looking for a place that they could buy some beer, a farm house or something and they got lost. And they didn't know where they were or where their camp was. So I told them where it was but then I was alone because they took off and there I was alone in the middle of France and night as black as black can be and guards with guns along the road and I didn't know what the pass word was. So I would call out and attract the guard and I would tell him, "I'm coming through and don't shoot." He would then tell me about where the next guard was. So here I was going alone with my rifle and grenades to hunt Germans in the middle of the night, all by myself. Kind of stupid but what are you going to do? That's the army for you.

I finally come to a cross road and there was a big bunch of people there and girls too. These girls were the Free French and they were saboteurs for our side. They would fire on the German convoys to do as much damage as they could. In Normandy, the girls are Amazons. They are bigger then men. I was thinking that one of these girls could wrestle Brother Jim to the ground. They were so big. The men were small. So the men would drive the team and the women would do all the forking of the grain up on the wagons and do all the hard work. So here they were with bayonets and BARs over their shoulders and they had rounded up these Germans. These girls had rounded up these Germans and were taking them to the concentration camp. They met our boys there. So I mixed in with them as if nothing happened and we came back home to camp.

Well, we came to camp and it was a regular camp with barracks in it and had a wild commanding officer. He tried to march us like the Germans, goose step and all that. I guess he was scarred he would be shipped out to the German front lines and would have to get into a battle so he tried to be an extra-good commanding officer. He was very hard on the boys. This one time he brought us out for exercises, and of course we space out by sticking our arm out and were then at arms length from another guy. There is a command for that. I forgot now what it is. Anyway, we did this and did our exercises. He was jump'en around in front of us. Then he was going to discharge us soldiers but he forgot the proper command. And he would say one thing, then another. The sergeant would talk out of the corner of his mouth, (he was in line with us). He would say, "Don't move. Don't move. That's not correct." And so we would stand there. We wouldn't move. He would go through everything he could think of. His face was turning red, very embarrassed. Finally he said, "Sergeant take over command." The sergeant said, "Attention, dismissed." And he dismissed us all. The poor commanding officer went off with his head down.

We were assigned to that camp for a while and I couldn't get away from him. I would be on guard duty most of the time and stay up all night and you'd want to sleep during the day. Naturally you'd be tired. I'd lie down in my bunk and he would come and make me get up and make up the bed. He wouldn't let me sleep. The next night he would put me on guard duty again. And I went to the back of the barracks and laid down under the barracks and he come and he fished me out of there and tried to make me pick up papers on the parade ground there.

Anyway, that one day a group of us were cadres and were sitting around a little fire on the parade ground there and there was a French boy and he would bring us eggs. He called it, "erks" we would boil them in a cup over this little fire we had. He'd be waiting and then say, "I think the chicken laid some more eggs." And he would run and get us some more. I don't think we paid him for them. Anyway I didn't. The sergeant said, "We are getting pretty close to the front line and if we have to go fight, they will shoot at the person who has chevrons. He said, "I'm going to take mine off." And he was a Top Staff Sergeant. So he took his chevrons off and I had my T4 chevrons, Technician Sergeant and I took mine off. All the others did too, the Corporal and Sergeant.

Then here comes that wild commanding officer and he now thinks we are Privates. He starts holler'en, "What are you just sitting there for? Start picking up papers." There is a Blue Book in the army that tells what you can and cannot do and what the officers can do and cannot do. For instance, if they call you anything other then your last name you don't have to do it. And, you don't have to tell them what your name is either. I don't think so anyway. At any rate, he was hollering at us to pick up papers and the sergeant said, "No." I was surprised. He said, "Why not?" And the reply was, "We are all sergeants." If there is anyone lower rank then you then he is suppose to do the work. He's not supposed to ask us to do that kind of work. We all kind of bristled up and got some courage from him and we refused to do it too. He said, "If your cadres then you better sew those stripes back on or they'll be gone forever and you'll be privates." He took off like a wild man.

Work in Post Office

While I was there I was assigned to a post office. Can you imagine that? My letters were ABCD and the other guy would continue on until the whole alphabet was used. We would sort the mail with these letters. We had to sort them out. After a while you would get to know the people that were writing. They'd be sending post cards and stuff like that. Also the stationary, you'd become familiar with their stationary. So you hardly ever had to look at the address. That's why so many of these letters and packages that would come in with addresses so balled up and yet the post office delivers it. Because they get to know where it's supposed to go.

Sophie would send me boxes of fruit every once in a while and candy and so on. These packages would be broken into somewhere along the line things would be stolen out of there, like chocolate bars. But like a banana, Sophie would wax them and they'd look real good. I would peal back the skin and the banana would instantly turn black. It would rot right there, the minuet the air hit it. With any of the fruit, it would fall apart the minuet you would peal it.

He was Starting to Go Kind of Crazy

While coming from the post office, I met a young boy. He looked very young. He was in the ordinance. There was something wrong with his eyes. They looked funny. He was one of the boys that were picking up the corps and cataloguing them. He had been with it for a very long time. He was starting to go kind of crazy but he didn't know that. He said, "There's nothing wrong with me," He says, "They are sending me to Nice." That is a town on the southern side of France. It was like a resort along the Mediterranean Beach. I said, "They're sending you there?" He said, "Yeah. And how long have you been here?" I told him and he said, "Well, you're entitled too." I couldn't believe it.

Mediterranean Vacation

So I inquired about it. They said, "Yes, you get two weeks out there. You go down there and there will be no saluting. You're going to be free to recuperate." I didn't think there was anything wrong with me either but I was very glad to go. I went with a friend of mine by the name of Poloa. He was very a very very Christian boy. So I couldn't possibly get into trouble as long as I was with him. We went up there to the Mediterranean and there were these hotels. Hotel Nigreus is what they gave us. Beautiful beach but it was rocky with cobble stones. You couldn't walk barefoot; you had to have straw shoes. They had straw shoes. They were quite ingenious. The water was warm and of course very buoyant. There was a ship that was sunk about a quarter mile or farther out in the ocean. I wanted to get to that ship so one day I started swimming and I swam all the way up there. People were up on the deck sunning themselves and diving off the deck of this sunken ship. I thought I was a pretty good swimmer but it was the salt water that held me up.

We had a good time there. We went on a sail boat to Monte Carlo. We couldn't get in there. No one with an army uniform was allowed in Monte Carlo. There was a tale about the Navy ship that pulled in there. The captain of the ship went out there to gamble and he used the ships payroll. He lost it all. So he told them, "If you don't give me back the money I will go back to the ship and turn my guns on you and will blast you from the face of the earth." And they knew he was crazy enough to do it so they gave him all his money back. But then they passed a law that anyone in uniform can not come into this gambling casino.

So we had a nice day and for dinner the hotel would have a table for 4 and then there would be 4 waiters, one on each corner. They had black suits on but they had patches on them and they were real shiny because they hadn't had a new suit since the atrocities in that country. They didn't have any food either. We were eating regular army food. They would say, "Do you want a little more hash, Sir?" And they would spoon you out some more hash, and that bitter coffee. That's what we were eating, but that was all right.

Heating Ice Water for 50 Showers at Once

The army came up with showers. It was a truck with powerful pump on it and something that would heat the water. They could break the ice and then drop a hose into the water whether it was a lake, creek, river, or whatever it was. Then they had a row of shower heads. It was outside with just a curtain around it. Then a place to take off your clothes and run underneath this shower. It was maybe at least a dozen or maybe two dozen of these shower heads and the hot water was pouring down. Man, did that ever feel good! You could only stay there a certain length of time then you had to move out and another bunch would come in. I don't know what kind of machine they had that could heat the water that fast. But that sure was a dandy thing.

Well, we finally got away from that wild commanding officer. We were on our way, and even though we were closer to the front lines, I was glad to get away from him. This time, we were walking and it had been snowing and freezing for some time now. That winter was a bad one. But we were walking through these woods. There was a kind of trail through there. We were walking two-by-two and somebody started singing.

"I've got sixpences. Jolly, jolly sixpence. I've got sixpence to last me all my life. I have sixpence to spend and sixpence to lend and sixpence to send home to my wife, dear wife. I have no friends to grieve me. No pretty little girls to deceive me. I am happy as a king, believe me, as we go rolling, rolling home. Rolling home."

We were all singing away and it was the most beautiful woods I had ever seen in my life. It was all white and sparkling, like… like just out of this world. It wasn't like Christmas because Christmas would have green. But it was seasonal, close to Christmas. It was a pretty, pretty walk through there.

We were in camp there, and one evening we were sitting around. A couple kids came, a boy and a girl. They had an accordion with them. This accordion was big, full size. When the little boy was playing it all you could see was his head and his toes. The accordion was as big as he was. The little girl would dance and sing. Of course they would ask for cigarettes mostly, one for Papa one for Mamma, one for Sister, one for Brother.

They were experts at it. They could wheedle out anything. And their song was Lilly Marlene.

"Underneath the lamp post, by the barracks gate, darling I remember the way you use to wait. It was there that you whispered tenderly that you loved me and would always be the Lilly of the lamp light, my sweet Lilly Marlene.

Time would come for roll call. The time for us to part, darling I caress you and press you to my heart. There in the far off lantern light I held you tight. We kissed goodnight. My Lilly of the lamp light, my sweet Lilly Marlene.

Orders come for sailing somewhere over there. All confined to barracks was more then I could bear. Know you were waiting in the street. I heard your feet but could not meet my Lilly of the lamp light, my sweet Lilly Marlene.

Resting on a pallet, just behind the lines even thought we're parted your lips are close to mine. You wait where the lantern softly gleams. You fair face seems to haunt my dreams. My Lilly of the lamp light, my sweet Lilly Marlene.

I understand this song was to be used if the Germans lost the war, then the people would be more sympathetic toward the Nazi soldiers.

Back in the Trucks

Well, we were back in these trucks again and they would always draw fumes from the exhaust pipe of the truck. We would have our heavy shoes and over coats and just everything we could put on. We all had head aches but we would be heading out. And the frost would be just a'snapping all around. And all of a sudden all of these trucks came to a stop, right there on the road. I looked and there was a barracks there. And the barracks must have been full of children because every window was cluttered with children's faces. Some of the windows were broken too and they were looking out at us and cheering us on. We stopped, actually it was for dinner.

We hadn't eaten yet that day. We looked, and there was these nuns, (I think they were nuns). They were caring 15 gallon kettles. Maybe not that big, maybe 10 gallons of soup. A very big kettle. And it was barley soup. That is the best soup that I like, barley soup. And here they come. They stopped with this big kettle by our truck. There were several other big kettles coming along being carried by two nuns each. We come out there with our cups that held almost a quart and they filled them up with that hot barley soup. I never tasted anything so good. Homemade. So we gave them our dinner which was C rations. I don't know what it was. They had hash, baked beans, hotdogs and stuff like that in those little small cans. Then they had the second can like that and had 3 cigarettes in there, some hard candy and crackers. We used the crackers for bread. There was some coffee and toilet paper, was all in the other can. We gave it all to the nuns so they could share with their children. They were telling us that one of those V rockets came over them one time and knocked the corner of the barracks to smithereens but didn't hurt anybody. So they were really God sent, in a God forsaken times.

Nunnery

So off we would go. That evening we stopped by a little shack. I don't know if it was a schoolhouse or what and the cooks had already got there to the shack. They made oatmeal for us, a homemade dinner of oatmeal. It was kind of raining and snowing at the same time so we had to eat outside. I was standing on something, maybe a lump of snow so I could reach the window sill and I was eating with my mass kit on the windowsill and the rain and stuff kept filling it up so I could have all the oatmeal I wanted. I kind of think that the thing I was standing on was a corpse because there were corpses all over the place. The ordinance didn't have a chance to pick them up. The soldiers were moving so fast.

These 11th Armored Division that I was in now, was under General Patton. The trucks we were riding in were called half-tracks. They had the back part of them were like a caterpillar tractor and the front had wheels. They had high sides of iron, over your head almost. So that's what we were riding in. We had a 50 caliber machine gun over each cab for protection. So that's what we were in. Those were the fighting devices, those half-tracks. They would go just about anywhere. We still didn't really get one of them. We were still in our regular trucks with the canvas over the top. Those that gave us headaches. And what do you know? Lee was there with me. That little Chinese boy. He was planning on being an officer's mess and here we were almost in Germany already. I was looking out the corner at the landscape and I saw a leg sticking out an arm sticking out. I was telling Lee, "I think we are getting pretty close to the front lines because there are dead people out there." He said, "Oh, no, you must be mistaken. They wouldn't let dead people lay around like that." So he started looking and he started seeing these arms and legs.

Tape 5, Side B

Harmonica playing.

11th Armored Division

I think little Lee was getting pretty scared. I think he waited a little too long to get his job of serving the officers. I don't think they were serving officers in that area any how. I don't know whatever happened to him. That was the last time I ever saw him. Well, as night was coming on, we pulled into a little farm house area and stopped. The sergeant told the people in the house to go upstairs. It was a two story house. It was a grandpa, and ma and I imagine the mother and two kids. They all skedaddled upstairs and we took over the down stairs. One of the guys run some wires from the truck hooked up a bulb so we had some light. All around the walls we laid our sleeping bags. They weren't much of a sleeping bag. More like a light comforter. It had a zipper on one side so you could zip-up but most of the people cut the bottom open so they could stick their feet out. That way if they wanted to go someplace they just lifted up the bag and could walk around the barracks with the sleeping bag would be still on. They did not have to crawl out.

No Kindness Shown

Anyway, one of the people asked the sergeant if they could come down to get something to eat. The sergeant gave them permission. To me that was unusual because we were in somebody else's house but they probably were the enemy already. We shared our meager dinner with them, regardless of who they were. Ordinarily, we didn't. When we crossed over into Germany there was an abrupt change. There was no kindness shown. As we went through the countryside and some of the houses were destroyed, some of the people looked very furious at us. If they could, they would kill us right there on the spot.

Souvenir Hunting

There were dead people all around that farm house. The next morning they fiddled around with the engine, they were always fiddling around or tuning up the engine of our truck. It was the half-track that we were in now. They had switched us over. I wanted a parka, a white parka. I figured that with all that snow, they wouldn't see me if I were dressed in white. I wouldn't make such a good target if I had something white. That morning the sergeant said, "Do you want to go souvenir hunting?" I think his real motivate was that he wanted us to get use to seeing a battle field. So we went out a ways, behind the house. About every 20 feet or more there would be a body. Bodies would even be laying on the fence. Our troops tried to cross the barbed wire and they were mowed down. One of them had a white parka on and one of the boys said, "Hay, Walt there's a white parka for you." But I could see it didn't do this boy any good. So I didn't want it after that.

Like I said, the Germans were clean. The German bodies were clean shaven and their uniforms were clean. And the GIs... there were about equal GIs killed as the Germans killed. The Germans had all their equipment still there. Ordinance couldn't catch up. The sergeant said, "You can take anything you want." There were some nice pistols there. I imagine they had money and rings, watches, everything. But I wouldn't touch any of that stuff. I didn't see anybody else either. One of the reasons was that we were going into battle pretty soon and we knew it. If we were made prisoners and if they found, say a German Lugar on us, then they would assume we had killed one of their officers. That meant instant death for that person. That kind of discouraged anyone from taking anything. But that was the first real battle field I had seen. A very very vicious battle had taken place there to kill that many people.

Visit a Town, But No One was There

So the next day we pulled up a little farther, little farther. We made camp again and stayed a couple days and then went on some more. I got tired of hanging around there with all those guys so I took my rifle; I had noticed a town near there. I thought I would visit the town. It was already in the back of the fighting so I figured it was safe enough. I went back and nobody was there. The stuff was still in the stores. The windows were broken and the doors swung open. You could take anything you wanted again, all kinds of stuff… but I didn't. I wasn't interested in anything like that.

There was a church there and I wanted to see what it looked like. It was a monstrous thing, so high. The ceiling was built so high. The roof was so high. I went in there. I couldn't pray in there. Everything was taken out. The good stuff was taken out. They hid it somewhere. Plaster was all over. There was a hole in the roof. So I left the church and I was checking out some of the beautiful buildings around there. All empty. Suddenly a jeep pulled up and there were two MPs in it. They "invited" me to come along with them. So I got in and they took me to a Marshall. He was in a two story barracks. He held his meetings in the upper story, the upper floor. We went over there and I was hauled in. They quizzed me about what I was doing in the village.

They said, "Where's your gas mask?" I asked, "Are we expecting a gas attack, or what?" They said, "No". They went on to explain that each day they would designate what the soldiers should carry, that is, if he was really an American soldier. So this day we were all suppose to carry our gas masks. I didn't know where the heck my gas mask was. I hadn't seen it since, I don't know when. Maybe I never had one. Anyhow that is what they would do. They would have the ordinance come out with whatever would distinguish us from the Germans.

The Germans were now wearing American cloths and sabotaging everything they could to slow the American army up. They'd burn stacks of GI cans of gasoline. "Gasoline dumps," they called them. And they would set them on fire and the cans would fly all over the place. They would turn the signs around and screw them up so that you didn't know where you were going. They would run wires across the road that would catch people driving in a jeep underneath their chins. This would cut their heads off. They found jeeps like that with all the people's heads cut off. They didn't know what it was but when they found out what it was, they welded a bar straight up and down in front of the windshield. It would cut the wires, any wires that were there. Nasty business, nasty boys. So that's what the Marshall told me, anyway.

They didn't care much about me but while I was waiting, there were some boys sitting on the floor leaning against the wall. There was a back window that was open. This one GI sprung through that window and started running. An MP that was marching back and fourth was just as fast. The MP had his little rifle out and aiming at the soldiers back. No doubt he was a German soldier trying to get away. He came so close to being killed. The MP told him to come back and he came right back. He knew he was going to get killed. So they let me go back to camp again. I didn't do any more exploring that day.

Walked into a Bosh Meeting

But every once in a while I would break away and head into town by myself. This time, it was again, same thing, I was walking alone. The streets were vacant and no body was around. All the stores were open, you could help yourself to whatever you wanted but I didn't mess with it. I stood there in a doorway and across the street, I saw what I thought was an American soldier, alone too. He walked along and then he went down stairs. There was some stairs there off the sidewalk, leading down. I said, "aaaa, he found a place where there was cognac. I'm going to get some too." So I went down these stairs and sure enough, there were some barrels with planks across them and there were three women back there. And they had a pretty good stock of some bottles and stuff. So I asked for a bottle of wine.

She gave me a bottle of wine and I looked around and on the opposite side (this was in a basement) so on the opposite side, there was a row of chairs, two by two. There was probably, maybe 50, a platoon, of what I thought was American soldiers sitting in the chairs and their officer was lecturing them. I didn't think much of it. I was use to American soldiers, *only*. So I took my bottle of wine in the opposite corner. There was a window there. So I relaxed and had writing paper in my helmet and a pencil and my wife's picture was inside my hat; a nice big picture. I relaxed, took a swig and started writing some letters. It was a long time since I had a chance to write letters. Just the ideal place. But then, I don't know how much time passed, but maybe ½ hour, and one of these women came up. I looked around and the place was empty. She pointed to the now empty chairs and run her hands across her throat. And she pointed in that direction and told me that was, "bosh, bosh." Which meant Germans.

Though that town had been liberated by American soldiers, the Germans had lived there so long that they knew the people and were quiet intimate with them. So these Nazi soldiers were hiding out somewhere in the town or in those tunnels. They had American cloths on and they would do as much damage as they could. I wouldn't be surprised if they even got into our chow lines. But the strange thing was that I had my rifle and equipment and that they never killed me. I can't figure that out. When I left the bar it was dark outside. Not a person in sight and all of a sudden I heard this truck. It was really a'comm'en. So I jumped out and flagged it down. It was the last GI truck in that town. Apparently the Germans would occupy the town at night and the GIs would occupy it during the day. There were situations like that. So I swung up on the back of the truck and the driver tore out of there as fast as that truck could go.

You Will Soon Find Out!

So we'd load up and off we'd go again traveling. After a while, we turned into a drive-way. The buildings there were, well, if they were farm buildings then they were all together like a village.

And they would go to their farms from there. These little villages were all over the place. As we were pulling in, on either side of the driveway, the ordinance had stacked our boys, head to toe. And the stacks were bigger then cord wood piles. On both sides of the road, probably several thousand, maybe. Well, maybe not that much but it looked like an awful lot of them soldiers killed there and I know they weren't all picked up. So there was a lot, a lot of slaughter there. So we pulled in and there was a head quarters there. We went in and the guy was a Captain. A very nice guy. They had been fighting and had pulled back to reinforce and they had lost three Lieutenants.

The Sergeant was running the place, the company then. But this was a Captain. He introduced himself and asked me about myself. I told him that I was a cook and I wanted to cook. He said, "We don't lose any cooks." I said, "That's the idea of it." He said, "Well, if I need cooks I'll call on you." I know he was just soft paddling me. He said, "You go down that path and you'll find a little barn. Go there and meet your platoon and sergeant. Your going to be assigned to them so get acquainted with them." I located them and the building was full of hay and they were sitting there. They had a little stove and were flying some kind of meat on top of the stove. It smelled real nice. They were very quiet. They wouldn't talk. I tried to inquire about what is it like out there on the front line. He said, "You'll soon find out." That's all he would say. I asked, "What kind of meat you got there?" He pulled back a shelter half and they had two well dressed pigs hanging there. And one of the guys there would go and cut off some side pork and put it on the stove, salt and pepper it and they would be having a feast. While I was there an officer come he said, "Boys, I wouldn't be eating that meat. Those pigs have been out there among the dead people and that's what they've been eating. I would advise you not to eat those pigs." He went away and they, as if they never heard him, cut off some more steaks and put it on the stove, salt and peppered it and kept on eating.

So that was my platoon I met. I was getting so tired of digging those fox holes every night. There happened to be a deep, steep and narrow ditch there. I figured if I would lay my sleeping bag next to this ditch then if something started happening I could then just roll into this ditch and be safe. This was somewhat earlier; there was no snow on the ground yet.

Size 12 Boots

Two German planes came and they were flying at the height of the trees. They were practically brushing the trees and they were going fast. If they had opened up with their machine guns there wouldn't be anybody left because they came so fast that nobody could even shoot back at them. I couldn't even bat an eye and they were already past me. So that was a very bad idea and from then on I would dig a hole. So we got organized and packed everything up into the half-track and started out getting close to the lines again. Again, I got my head ache, cold, and miserable. They had given us some boots but they were all the same size, about size 12. Because we had been freezing our feet, they give us the size 12 boots and then a truck came in with blankets. A little black man was driving it and was he ever a truck-driver! He wheeled in there and the blankets were like Swiss cheese. The Germans had opened up with a 50 caliber on him. He out ran them but they riddled the bundles of blankets and they were no good.

They All Went to Sleep

I took mine and cut out the good pieces and sewed them onto the inside of my jacket to make my jacket a little warmer. We were really freezing out there and then they gave us the size 12 boots. Oh, Man, they were difficult to maneuver in. So we were going with this half-track and eventually come to a stop for the night. Everybody was told you don't need to be digging fox holes because we are going again early. They didn't tell us yet that we were going to attack. They just said not to dig fox holes. And me! They told me to climb up on top of the truck behind the 50 caliber machine gun. They had set out some flares in front of the truck and said if you see one of these flares and see anybody there then open up with the machine gun because there isn't suppose to be anybody in front except the enemy. They then all went to sleep.

There I was. I don't know why they did that to me all the time. I knew while I was sitting up there on the truck against the sky line, anyone down below could spot me up there. And the enemy was very good with a knife too. They could throw the knife or sneak right up to someone who was sleeping. You'd think it was a buddy of yours and then they would cut your throat. They silently killed as many as they could and that is why those guys would open up the bottom of the sleeping bag, so they could move fast if they had to. But anyway, I wasn't about to sit there behind that 50 caliber machine gun. I didn't even know if I could operate the darn thing. I didn't have any experience with it. So I got down by the front wheel of the truck, right next to the ground and leaned against the wheel there. I put my rifle at, "ready" and I'd listen and that's how I kept guard during the night.

Next morning we were still alive and moved along the line with our trucks and all. We got into a different position and again, when evening came, we all stopped. This time they said that I didn't have to sit up there next to the 50 caliber. Everybody else bedded down. They told me to walk guard. There was quite a bit of snow now, kind of crunchy, hard. These size 12 boots were hard to walk in, especially trying not to make noise. I was supposed to walk the parameter between the enemy and our soldiers while they slept. I was to meet a guard, then turn around to walk until I met still another guard. If I didn't meet a guard then I was suppose to give an alarm because he would have been killed or destroyed somehow and the enemy would have broken through. So I started walking, scrunch, crunch, crunch on the snow in a half-moon lit night.

I began to see enemies all over the place, the shadows. How could you see anything? So I would stop behind a tree, look around wait, and then I would move up a little. All that night I never saw another guard anywhere. I knew they were goofing off someplace. I knew they weren't killed. At least I didn't think they were but I never met them. This went on until probably 2 in the morning and the Sergeant come up and says, "You don't have to walk anymore. Go back to the truck. They are parked in the woods and get your mess kit and the cook prepared you some hot oatmeal. And then we're going to attack."

We are Going to Attack

I said, "oh, man." and sat down on a log. And my belly felt like it was full of worms churning around in there. Maybe more like snakes. I could visualize putting on the bayonet and charging into the enemy with it like on that calendar we got from Canada. Finally, I got myself together and tried to find my truck in the woods. I kept looking and finally found it. Like I said, the truck beds were steel boxes maybe 4 or 5 feet high and hard to get into but to get my mass kit I did it. I was pretty hungry by then. I located my mass kit and of course I had my rifle in my other hand and tried to climb down the side of the truck and I fell down and lucky my big size 12 boot got caught up there. I didn't crush down to the ground but was hanging. I had two hands but both were full and I had to drop something and like a darn fool I dropped my rifle. I scrambled back up the truck, released my foot but the rifle had hit the mud and was dirty now. The best it would do was shoot three times and then it would jam. And here we were attacking and no time to clean that darn thing in the dead of night. Anyway, I got some oatmeal and we started out walking, two at a time.

The Germans would be shelling with a railroad gun. Those are monsters. The shell must be as big as a cream can or something because when the shell would be coming at you it would be spinning and throw sparks coming through the air. But you didn't know where it was going to land. Imagine what would happen... so we would hit the ground, hit the snow. And each times you hit the snow you would scrap more snow into those big boots. They were laced up but not tight enough. We kept on a walk'en, struggling along until day light was coming. And then there was a bombardment. I don't know if it was rockets or what. Everybody hit the ground and scampered. There was a road that we were walking parallel to. There was ice all over the place and there was a little two foot bank there so I jumped over the bank onto the road. While I was laying there another guy came running down the road and he laid down next to me so I would be like his log. I would get the bullets that were meant for him. It made me mad but I looked around and saw I was laying right in the middle of a mine field. Those little copper wires, there were three wires sticking up out of the ice. Thank god they were frozen in so hard that they didn't work. They didn't push down to activate the mine. I think that is the only reason they didn't go off there. We certainly must have been tramping on them. But sometimes you win.

We kept on a-go'en. There was a guy sitting there on a bank, at one time he was alive. Both his legs were shot off and he had put his belt around one leg and some kind of a handkerchief around the other and twisted it up. He was frozen in that position. Every once in a while we would run into a live GI who would be yet somehow guarding the road. He'd be in a fox hole, right up to his chin. He would be sitting there with a 50 caliber machine gun. He was backing us up in case we ran into trouble.

There was another company marching to the right of us. I didn't know how close we should be to that other company so I asked the Sergeant. He said, "Why don't you kind of fill in between the two companies?" I said," alright." But then we come to a woods and one company went on one side of the woods and the other company went on the other side of the woods. So what am I to do? So I started through the woods. I kept looking up into the trees because sometimes there would be snipers up there. They would have on a perforated onion or potato sack only green. Their hands would be painted green and they would have green cloths and I'll be darn, but you couldn't see them up there all green. I didn't want to be behind them. I was sincerely walking along but not too fast. I didn't mind if those companies got a little ahead of me. Then something happened. One of our artillery shells, (I think my brother Ted was operating the artillery behind us) was short cycle. Somebody didn't put enough power in there and so it was about to fall among our own soldiers. The shell was cutting off the tops of the trees like you would with an ax. Bam! Bam! And the trees would be falling down. And that shell kept right on a go'en but not very far. It then hit the ground and it exploded. Woof! A concussion! It lifted me right out of the air. I looked and it made quit a hole there. You could drive a truck into it. I said, "To heck with this. This isn't any safer then going with the rest of the guys." So I put on a little speed and caught up with them.

They were on the perimeter of a hill. Not quite to the top but about 2 or 3 feet from the top. Anyway, if you crawled around close enough to the ground the shells would go over your head. Our guys were all spread out along the hill, up and down too of course. They were quite deep. This was across the Dragon's Teeth, The German Dragon's Teeth. Beyond the Dragon's Teeth were bunkers that looked like Eskimo houses. There was a slit in them and I imagine each one had an 88 in there which is a very vicious gun that the Germans had. Much better then anything we had. They could cover the field with this gun but our sappers had gone there ahead. They had bandoleers that were like rakes, a hand rake and across the top was the explosive charge. Two guys would sneak up on the Eskimo house each had a BAR, (that's a high powered rifle) the shells were like a 50 caliber, maybe a little smaller. I don't know how many they had, maybe 20 each.

They would station themselves and would be shooting into this slip so nobody could zero in on us. Then the sappers would sneak up there with the bandoleers and prop them up against the hole with the explosive charged. They would set it off and run and it would blow the top off and blow up whoever was inside. I don't know who or what was inside but the French had those kinds of things too. The French had an underground railroad running to supply their bunkers. I suppose the Germans had the same thing. I never got in to see them. Anyway we were able to cross the Dragon's Teeth. They were like dominos setting up on end. They were made of very very solid concrete. When you were among them you felt safe. The bullets would just fly away. The bullets would hit the domino and zing off someplace.

All of a sudden the Sergeant grabbed me, "Where the heck were you?! I'm going to court marshal you. They're going to shoot you." Anyway he had sent my squad to reconnoiter. Everybody was laying there in their fox holes holding the position while my gang had to go forward to find out where the Germans were. I didn't think they went very far. Maybe just over the hill into some bushes and sat down for a while, which was a typical way. Nobody was crazy enough to go charging out there. Anyway, I don't know because I didn't go with them. There was an empty fox hole that was dug by someone who was either killed or wounded, most likely wounded. They had vacated it. It was only about a foot and half deep. That's all. The ground was frozen like cement and yet there was a trickle of snow that was now melting during the day and running in there. So all I could do was scrap out a corner a little deeper with my bayonet.. Then I could sit there with my cup and bale it out so I wouldn't have to sit in the water, only the mud. I took my gun apart there in the mud and wiped it off the best I could. I didn't trust it very much. It would shoot but kind of a slow chug, chug, not a snap like it was supposed to but it was better then nothing.

Then these mortar shells started coming, coming like a son-of-a-gun. I was checking out, where the heck were they coming from? Then I spotted them. There was a woods and at the corner of the woods I could see smoke just before the shell would hit. I surmised I could see some action there. The Germans had the mortar but they couldn't shoot in the woods so they had to have it out in the open; but very close to the woods. So I alerted the officer or whoever he was, I didn't know. He gave an order, "Everybody fire 5 rounds at the corner of the woods." This was for effect. So there were 200 men shooting 5 rounds a piece into that corner of the woods. Needless to say, we didn't get anymore mortar shells from them. But man, it must have been like a hail storm, all of a sudden down upon their heads.

I didn't have any partner; just me and the fox hole. Then the Sergeant brought a guy over. His partner had been killed. A shell fell into his fox hole and exploded but he wasn't killed just shell shocked because of exposure to his buddy being killed.

Tape 6, Side A

Harmonica playing *Little Redwing*.

A Missile Took a Cigarette From my Mouth

Usually there was camaraderie with a partner but this guy wouldn't talk, or couldn't talk. He'd just laid against the bank there and let the water come. He wouldn't bail it. He'd just lay there. The other guys who had a partner, one would sleep while the other would watch so nobody could creep up on you with a knife or whatever. But I couldn't. I had to stay up all night by myself. I had to sit up there, bail water and try to sleep at the same time. Oh, boy! Well in the morning I kind of realized I had no help and lit up a cigarette and was sitting there in a corner, with all the water bailed out. The guy still wouldn't talk. After you've been there a while, you could hear the shells and could tell whether they were our shells or enemy shells coming. Usually you had an opportunity to duck below the ground level. So you kept alert but this time there was an explosion to my right, pretty close and I started ducking forward and, ZING! A missile come and took the cigarette right out of my mouth and slammed right into the side of the fox hole. It made a hole about the size of my wrist. I don't know how far it went with my cigarette. I had become pretty fast at ducking. I was fast but…if I was a little faster that thing would have taken my head off. It only took my cigarette…this time. So I asked the Captain, "Why are we hanging around? Why don't we go ahead?" And he said that the other companies hadn't caught up to us yet, on either side. They were experiencing some great resistance. The Germans were doing everything they could to keep us from going ahead. They were really protecting their Hitler.

I Want my Coffee

We didn't have anything to eat. I had one can of something but the thing broke off on the lid and there was no way in the world you could open that can. I don't know what was in there. After a while, the Corporal came over and he said, "Come with me and we will go down and get some rations. Get some stuff." And so about 8 of us got together. We would start down that hill and we'd go about 20 feet and here comes that shell and we would hit the ground. But lucky the ground was thawed out somewhat. Maybe 6 inches or a foot was thawed out and those shells would go into this mud or wet sand and then they would hit the frozen dirt before they would explode. They were kind of muffled and they would splatter us with the mud.

We kept go'en at her about 20 feet and then hit the ground and that thing would splatter at us again but we got down below the dragon's teeth again and it wasn't so bad. We kept on a-go'en, a-go'en and it was getting dark. There were mines around and we sure hoped the Corporal knew where he was taking us. Eventually we got to some trucks and they had thermoses of coffee. There were at least 5 gallons in there, maybe more in thermal cans. So 2 or 3 of us would take hold of the handles, (they had handles on them) and we would walk with them. They contained hot coffee and oh, man, I wanted a cup of hot coffee so badly. So I suggested, "Could we drink our coffee now?" And I thought they would court marshal me on the spot. We weren't supposed to ask that. We were supposed to wait our turn and not dig into the rations ahead of the rest of the soldiers. So we carried these things. Some of us were also caring boxes of rations about the size of a cherry lug on our shoulders. It was nailed on all sides and it had those cans in it. So here we were walking along and we come to a road that shouldn't have been there and the Corporal said, "You guys stay here. I don't know where we are. We don't want to walk into a mine field. I'm going to go scout around and find the trail we had come on so we can get back to the front lines." So he went.

Counter Attack

And then, wouldn't you know, the German started shelling that road with phosphate. Phosphate is a chemical that if it gets on your skin, it just keeps on a'goen and will burn right on through. The only way to stop it is if you are in a barrel of water and covered yourself with water. That would stop it from burning. The shell would go off like a fireworks right in the middle of the road. SPLATTER! We were lying there, without our Corporal, sweating it out. There were banks of snow all around and when the next shell came it was a little closer and the third one would come closer yet. As it come closer, I'm crawling into the snow bank and burying myself in it. I don't know if it would help but boy, I didn't want that phosphate. They only shot off about 4 of them and then they stopped. Eventually here comes our Corporal. Yes, he found the way.

So we started walking with these boxes and every few feet we would hit the ground. Gravel and shrapnel would splatter against the boxes we were carrying and against our thermos jugs but we would get up and go some more. Eventually we got back to our troops on the line and it was pitch dark. They opened up one of the thermos cans and had the guys sneak up there with a cup and they would give them a cup full of the hot coffee. Well, guess where my cup was. Back in my fox hole and I didn't have it with me. I had been bailing water with it and I left it there. I wanted my coffee! There were some boxes lying around there. They looked like cracker-jack boxes and I imagined they were waxed, probably from rations of some sort. So I picked one of them up. I shook the dirt out and I went over to get my coffee in that. He started pouring the coffee and that hot coffee opened up the bottom and all the coffee dumped out on the ground and the sergeant said, "Move on. You've had your share." Man! I didn't get nothing! No rations. No coffee. I was kind of disgruntled. So I went over to find my fox hole and yup, that guy, my new partner was sitting there with water up to his bum. Nobody bailed it out and I just couldn't get in there. I just couldn't do it anymore.

I was standing up and looking down into that mess and ZING-O! A shell exploded and I didn't duck and a chunk of fragment of that shell went into my leg, by my groin on the inside. It just missed the bone. It went in and out the other side. God made a channel through there. And if I had been down on my knees baling, like a good solider should have been, it would have gone right through my heart. But I was laying down now all right. Medic. I heard him coming. He was like a St. Bernard, with a sack around his neck. And he's bitching, he says, "I didn't want to fight and look what they did. They made me a medic. Now everyone's got a fox hole except me and I got to go walking around on the outside of the foxholes. With all this shelling, I know, I know I'm going to get hit."

But he came up to where I was. He took a rag and wrapped it around my leg and gave me a shot and went away. So I was laying there. I didn't go into the fox hole but kept laying there where I dropped along side. I didn't want to get in that water anyway. Toward morning a sergeant came, maybe it was 12 o'clock or one. He made his way up there. He says, "We can tell by the way they are shelling, it looks like they will counter attack and they will be trying to drive us back. And they might come with tanks. We have one bazooka here. So we'll put the bazooka up front and will fight off the tanks with it while the rest of us dig down a little deeper into the fox holes if we can.

But he says, "For you, you are free. if you want to get down below the dragons teeth by yourself the medics will come." The real medics wouldn't come up there because it was too dangerous with the mines and all. "If you can get down there by yourself then you're free to go." And off he went. Boy, I wanted to get out of there. I didn't want to be there after a counter attack. Good god! Them two guys trying to hold back those tanks. That would have been something. That bazooka, half those shells wouldn't explode even. We had tested them out on some logs and half of them wouldn't explode. So anyway, I started crawling but I wasn't making any headway. I looked and would still be practically in the same place. But I must have got to another fox hole and a head came up and asked, "What's the matter?" I said, "I'm hit and I'm trying to get down there where the medics will come." He says, "Well, I'll help you." And he crawled out of his safe hole, (relatively safe) to help me. And so between him and me, I could walk on one leg and we would walk a ways and drop to the ground, walk and drop as the shells would be peppering us.

He took me down to where the dragon's teeth were and set me behind one of them. The shells would be pounding the dragons tooth but they couldn't get through to where I was sitting. I was safe except if one hit in front. It seemed like all the shells would land down below the hill at the bottom. Beyond the dragons teeth, he found a guy in a fox hole. A nice deep one. Oh, it was 5 feet deep, a big one and he was there alone. He asked him if he would mind if I stayed there until the medics came. He said that it would be all right. So I crawled in there and I took out that can I was trying to open. Neither one of us could open that darn thing. We smashed it all up but couldn't open it. But he had some water so that was good to have a drink. I don't know if I slept or it was that dope the medic gave me but anyway morning come and sure enough here comes the medics.

A medic isn't supposed to be armed, you know. They have that Red Cross on them and are the good guys. And here they come with burp guns. That's what the tank crew has, short guns that fire very rapidly. And each medic was armed with those machine guns. So they brought a stretcher and told me to lay down on the stretcher and they laid those machine guns on top of me and then they would hook on to carry me. And then a shell would come and they would drop me to the ground. Everybody would drop to the ground. Then they would pick me up and carry me some more. Finally we got to a jeep, it was dark out again. So it must have been all day and I didn't know where I was. Anyway, they put me on a jeep, somehow with the stretcher and hauled me to a first aid station. This first aid station was one of the old country cow barns and of course there were no cattle in it but there were still the cow-stalls and the soldiers were laying on the ground where the cows use to stand. And they had blankets hung over the windows to keep the light out. There was one doctor and one medic. They must have been boozing it up or something because they were laughing and joking around. Then they took a knife and zip, with a scalpel and cut my boot from top to bottom.

And I hollered at him, "I waited for these boots. You can't get boots up there in the front. And here you're cutting my boot up." He said, "Well, that's the way we do it." And the fragment of shell that had hit me was in that boot but I didn't ask for it. I started shivering and I couldn't stop. I was shivering! I never shivered like that in my life. And another thing, the enemy rockets were coming. It was just like a freight train up in the air, a whole bunch of rockets fired at one time. They are on a truck and there are several trucks and they blast all of them and then run with them trucks so our artillery cannot fire back on them. Apparently the blankets fell off the windows and the lights were shining, the flash lights mainly, there was no electricity. And the doctor who wasn't so jolly now he said, "What the heck, they're getting closer and closer." The Sergeant said, "I think the blankets blew off with the last time they shot." Well for god sake put them back up again!!!

Get the Heck Out and Surrender Yourselves

Eventually an ambulance came and they put a bunch of us in the ambulance and started hauling us farther away from the lines. And I got to talking with them people in the ambulance and it was my Captain in there from my original company. And

I said, "What the heck are you doing here?" And he said, "A grenade went off in my hand." I said, "How is it?" He said, "It burns like the dickens." He was telling me that he couldn't get the scouts to go out ahead of the company and he didn't want them to keep walking without knowing where the enemy was. So he went out himself scouting ahead of the company. He was quite a Captain to do a thing like that. He said, "I had my big gloves on, a radio in one hand and a carbine over my shoulder, (a little short rifle). He says, "I ran into a fox hole full of Germans and they had a machine gun there." I said, "What the heck did you do?" "I couldn't get my gun," he says "so I just jumped in there and started kicking them in the butt and hollering, "get the heck out" and surrender yourselves. We got you surrounded all around now you surrender yourself to the GIs over there." They listened to him because he was a commanding officer and they were use to listening to commanding officers. They didn't realize that there was a difference. But they listened to him and lucky for them that they did because they would have all gotten it.

While we were there in the fox hole, before I got hit, there was a guy that came up to the top of the hill and everybody started aiming their guns at him. He was a Nazi German that had come up there. He wanted to surrender but he was afraid that we would shoot him. There was a bunch them (Germans) and they forced this guy up there. I don't know if they drew straws or what because he was a crying and ringing his hands. He thought for sure he was going to die. I could see all that and I kept hollering at our guys, "Don't shoot! Don't shoot!!" After a while he got a little braver and he waved his arms and hollered down there and a whole bunch of guys came out with their hands above their heads to surrender. If we had shot the original guy then the others would have fought to the end. Lucky that nobody pulled the trigger. I was kind of surprised. I thought someone would. Anyway this Captain got those German guys to come out of there and he saved their skin.

Relax, It's Good for You

We got to another hospital and this one was a real hospital. All this time the medics were boys and they were very good nurses.

I guess the second or third hospital I suspected that there was a woman there; a woman nurse. Because they had a mask over their face and only their eyes would stick out and their head was wrapped up in some type of cloth and he or she took my privates and wrapped them up in the back so the doctor could get at that wound hole. He ran some kind of stick through that hole from one end to the other. He hit a nerve and holy mackerel! I never hurt that hard in my life. But he had to rod it out somehow. That nurse that saw me, I could not tell if it was a boy or a girl and I was so embarrassed because I wasn't use to a woman there doing that kind of work. And I was looking and she could read my mind and she was laughing behind that mask. Her eyes were laughing but I couldn't see her mouth. So I think it was a girl.

Anyway eventually, we kept moving back to bigger hospitals. And in one hospital there was a whole row of beds, all the way from one end of the hospital to the other. The nurses had carts and would come by and they would give us a shot. Then just the time we were ready to go to sleep, here comes that darn cart again. And they gave you another shot, and you couldn't sleep. Oh, I wanted to sleep so badly. Finally, this nurse came to me and she ran out of shots. She said, "I'll go back and send somebody over with it." So another nurse came and I said, 'No, it's not me. You want to go to the other end of the room." And you know, she believed me. She went there and she gave the other guy my shot. I could hear him hollering, "Errr, Errr." And she said, "Relax, it's good for you. It will make you well." And she gave him another shot. A couple days later, I walked over there to the other side to see who the guy was. I wasn't going to apologize or anything because I knew he would get up and kick my butt. He was an army tank driver. The tank caught on fire and he was brunt all over his whole body and he was in a cast. His whole body was in a cast and where the mouth was, there was a hole there. That's all. Just like a jack-o-lantern. He's the guy that that got my shot. I hope it helped him.

We'd lay there awake at night. The GIs couldn't sleep and they'd be telling their experiences and if a man wanted a story, man, he should have been there to take it down. There are things that I heard there that would make your hair stand up on end.

There were these two guys, they were machine gunners and they dug a fox hole. And then they found a door someplace and put it on top of them. Then they covered the door with dirt and crawled in there. They had a slit there where they could have the machine gun sticking out. They said, when the Germans were charging they wouldn't stop for nothing. They would empty that machine gun, empty the belt, slip another one in there and fire that gun until it would get red hot. It wouldn't shoot then. They had to take the barrel out then and replace it with a cool barrel while the Germans were coming. And then they tried to hold them back with the machine gun. Can you imagine walking into the face of a thing like that? But the Germans did it.

This one guy was digging mines. Digging out mines on the road and he had a crew of two or three. It was a new type of mine and they didn't know how to put the safety on so they would just dig the mine out of the dirt and carefully stack it along side the road. He had told us that while still on the ship, the boys tried to talk him into going to confession but he said, "No, God will never forgive me for what all I did." But they pestered him and talked him into it. He carried that mine. It exploded and it cut him in half. The guy that was with him loaded up the jeep and just left him there. He then told the ordnance where he was.

When the guy, his name was Gil, got back from digging the mines, he didn't have time to dig a hole but there was a guy that had a nice hole. He didn't like him really but thought maybe he could stay over night so he asked him, "Can I stay over night with you?" That guy said, "Yes. I got two ledges and you can use one of them." There were two ledges of dirt in the hole. Gil started spreading his blanket out or his sleeping bag, but the guy said, "No, no. I want to sleep on that side." And Gil said, "What's the difference? I already got my sleeping bag." "Well it's my fox hole and it seems like I ought to have the right to sleep where I want to." So Gil took his bag on the other side then. That night, Bed Check Charlie came by. It was a German photographic plane. It would take photographs but it would go so high that we couldn't shoot at it so people just left it alone. Bed Check Charlie seldom did anything but this night he started dropping bombs, dropped one bomb and then another one closer and the third one hit that fox hole. It split it right open and mangled the body of that guy that owned that fox hole. Gil said, "I picked him up and carried him to the medic tent and every bone in his body was shattered."

The Jeep Flipped Over

Then there was this tank corps. They had been scraping there and then pulled back for reloading. It was hot in the tank so they all took a break. One guy that was operating the tank laid down in front of his own tank for a rest. Apparently it was shady there. His buddy came alone with his tank and didn't realize where his friend was. He thought maybe he was still inside. I don't know what he realized but he gave that tank a little shove. You know how jolly people are and he ran the tread of the tank right over the guy's belly. The buddy was real mad. His eyes, you could see he was mad in his eyes. He had gone through so much. They called a medic and gave the guy a shot of poison. It killed him right there on the spot.

This other guy was a cavalry man. I wanted to be in the Cavalry because I thought it involved horses but the modern Cavalry didn't. Our Cavalry had a jeep first of all and then an army tank and one of the trucks. And those three had to reconnoiter a head of the regular army that would be fighting the Nazis. They had to go ahead to let us know what we would encounter and how we were going to squash it. When I had first noticed the Cavalry guy, he was riding with us on a truck, and we were headed closer to the front lines and he wanted to get back to his outfit. He had a carbeen instead of a regular M1 rifle like we had. We had 7 shots, semi automatic and his was a little carabeen. It had about 10 shots. I noticed he had attached another magazine to the first magazine so he could just jerk it out turn it around and he would have 10 more shots on that little gun. When we were riding along, the natives, they all were armed one way or another, would salute us by firing into the air. So during this volley of shots the Cavalry guy whipped his gun from over his shoulder and had it over the side of that truck ready to pulverize those people. He thought they were shooting at us. He was really that quick.

He was telling me later that he was in this Cavalry jeep. He had a driver and they were driving along and were the first ones out. On the cross roads the Germans would have an 88 zeroed in on the cross roads. He had just passed the cross-road and the 88 opened up on him and a bullet zipped over their heads. They were too close. So the Germans fired another shot and it was too short. It hit in front of them. So they knew they were backed in and the 3rd shot was going to get them. They couldn't turn around so the driver put the jeep in reverse and he just jumped on it for all it was worth. They were going backwards and he was going to veer off the road but the jeep flipped over and that's the last he remembered. When he woke up he was in the hospital. He wanted to find out what happened to the rest of his crew so he was anxious to get back to the front lines. Actually, there were many GIs in the hospital that couldn't wait to get back into the fighting. And they would sit on a fence there by the hospital and watch the trucks go by and they would holler, "Where are you from?" If the jeep or truck was going to their outfit they would jump off the fence and their bandages would be a flying but they would jump on the truck and off they'd go to the front lines. They were so anxious to keep on a'goen. They were anxious to get on to Berlin.

These two guys at the hospital, their tank had been burned up. The gasoline ignites fast. The Germans had diesel in theirs that didn't ignite so fast. But the boys were kind of on their feet already. They didn't see any trucks coming so they started hitch hiking back to the front lines. A tank column came by and they asked, "Can you use a couple more tank operators?" They said, "Oh, yea, come along." Ours were little tanks compared to the Tiger tanks the Germans had. Our little tank spotted a German Tiger tank coming down the rail road track and they whipped the gun around, a 44 mm or something like that and they blazed away at the Tiger. It would have been better if they just sit still. Finally the big tank turned its cannon around that they were carrying around and one blast shattered the small tank and it killed the two hitch hikers. It only took one shell to penetrate the tank.

The bazooka shells, Sophie wondered how they could shoot through iron. These bazooka shells could go through iron. They could go through about 4 inches of steel. The bazooka shell looked like an inverted funnel. It would hit and what ever was in there, I don't know what it was, but it would start burning. And it was like a sadoline torch and it would burn a hole through the iron. I don't know about 4 inches, maybe less. Maybe in the front of the tank it would be that heavy. But that's how it worked. You could stop a tank with a bazooka shell which was about the size of a thermos bottle. You could propel the morter farther or closer by how many charges you put in. A charge looked like the little packets of sugar sweetener. That's what it looked like and how many you added, that's how far it would go. You'd put it into a thing that looked like a little 4 inch stove pipe. You'd drop them in and then drop the shell in there and the thing would really take off.

I probably told you the time I got tired of digging a fox hole and I laid down next to a a deep trench-like thing. I should have crawled down in there but there was water down in there. I figured if something was stirring I could roll into that ditch. I just got comfortable and two German planes came over and they were coming at tree-top level. Coming like a son-of-a-gun. And they come and they went and I was still laying there with my mouth open. I could not even bat an eye they came so fast. If they had been firing I'd been like a sieve laying there on top of the ground.

The War was Slowly Coming to an End

I was getting pretty well healed up and the war was slowly coming to an end then the Germans made their final charge there and Brother Ted was saying how they were firing their cannons. He was firing his cannon in a circle because they were all around him. Eventually the thing came to an end. They sent me to Le Havre which was a fort there on the French border. It was a dandy port. The Germans were going to attack England Le Havre so they were building plywood boats, bunches of them. The boats were about 6 inches thick, laminated plywood. I don't know if they had torpedoes on them or how they were armed but what happened, they were using the Frenchmen for labor there. Bob was telling me. Bob was a sailor who sailed to New York and back. He was French but learned English so he was helping us cook.

We would get into conversations. He was a native of Le Havre. He said that they had to work for the Germans and but were treated pretty good. If you needed coal, they would give you a half a sack of coal. He had this bicycle. They all had bicycles, those that could afford them. These bicycles had high wheels and trailers. Anyway, Americans and British would fly planes and drop notes telling the French to get out of there because we were going to bomb that place. They did that 3 days in a row. They told them exactly what day they were going to bomb it so the French could get out of there. Well the Germans wouldn't let them out. They figured as long as the Frenchmen were there we wouldn't bomb the place. But we did. And we killed enormous amount of French. So French were a little resentful to Americans because of that. They had a whole big grave yard full of French people there.

This Bob was saying he put his mother on the trailer and started paddling out of there and the guards stopped him. "Where you going Bob?" He says, "You're not supposed to leave." And Bob says, "Oh, I'm just going over the hill to take my mother back. I'll be right back."

Tape 6, Side B

Washing German Mines

We moved into a fort that was near LaHarve and I'd go down there along the beach and pick up German and French money, silver and whatever souvenirs. There was a guy with a Belgian horse, a huge animal, and a two wheeled wagon. It was a dump wagon. He was cleaning out areas where there use to be roads with that horse and hauling the bricks away. That's all I'd seen; that one man working away. There was a woman an old lady and she had a wheeled buggy. It was a box with buggy wheels on it and she would go down to the beach and she would pick out those crustaceans. I don't know what the heck they were. They were about an inch or two across and she would load that buggy up. She had two dogs that were tied up to the axel underneath that wagon box. They were unmatched set of dogs. One looked like a hound and they would help her pull that wagon around. They would pull with all their might. Their feet would be a' slippen and they would be a'pullen that thing. When she would see some GIs, she would stop that wagon and they would come up and buy that stuff, those crustaceans. The GIs would break them open right there and eat them. They did but I never did. It must have been pretty good stuff.

I was assigned a kitchen. I wasn't cooking; I was just in charge of it. I made sure that it was operable during the night. We would make a bunch of cheese sandwiches or just bring bread and cheese out and whoever was hungry could come in there and have something to eat. My crew was a bunch of German POWs. There was about 12, a squad. Usually there would be one guy that could speak English, probably an officer. I would tell them what I wanted done, the place cleaned up, dishes washed, sinks cleaned and he could take over from there. I didn't have to do a thing and it would be an excellent job. They would do a number-one job. Sometimes they were washing German mines.

The mines were glass mines that were shaped like a bowl and we used them for cereal. Cereal bowls. One time I asked one of them, "Do you know what this is?" They said, "noooo, nien." He knew darn well they were German mines. A mine detector couldn't be attracted to glass. When these mines would go off, the doctors had the darnedest time trying to pick that glass out of your body. Anyway, that was in the past. I liked working with them guys, they were real good. I didn't have to bother with them at all. One of them came over once and asked if he could dig dandy lion greens. It was getting spring time. I said, "Sure, if you get some for me too." So he went, picked them, cleaned them up nice, put oil and vinegar on them and we had a feast of fresh greens.

I had trouble one time. A drunken staff sergeant came up. A staff sergeant is almost a lieutenant already. They are way up there. He wouldn't eat the cheese sandwiches, he wanted fried steaks. And I said, "No. you can't have steak." He got tough with me. Oh man, he was going to pull rank on me. He got mad, lifted up his fists and wanted to fight with me. I didn't want to fight. Anyway, one of the Germans came up and asked, "Do you want us to take care of him for you?" Man, I only had to say the word and they would have pulverized that guy. I knew what they would do but I finally was able to kick him out and locked the door. He would be pounding on the door and windows and was running around. So the next day I told the commanding officer that the staff sergeant was going to pull rank on me for his steaks when I told him he could not have steaks.

"I don't give a darn who comes up there." The commanding offer said. "I put you in charge, and you're in charge and nobody else." I knew where the staff sergeant slept and I went over there. He was still in bed and I woke him up and said, "Ok. Your not drunk anymore, I'll fight you. Let's go behind the barracks." He probably would have knocked the devil out of me because I wasn't in too good of a shape after coming from the hospital. But I had to do something. He chickened out and apologized the best he could. So I didn't have any problem with him after that.

Sometimes I would go on a hike with the guys just for exercise. We were walking along the country side and I found those white mushrooms. So I kind of let the others go ahead and then went over and slipped out through the fence. The mushrooms had pink bottoms, exactly like we had to home. So I started picking them and putting them in my canteen pouch and pockets. They were all over the place and soon I was loaded down. Before I had left the kitchen there was a bunch of Polish soldiers, about 12. 12 was a squad. They were sitting around the fire. They were waiting for a Polish truck to come and pick them up. They'd been waiting there for about a week already. So I got a can of bacon. They had a frying pan and I gave them the bacon and then I went for the exercise walk with our guys. So when the guys were done with their exercises and were on their way back, I kind of jumped behind them and marched in. I then went over to those Polish guys and I asked them, "Are these mushrooms any good? We have them to home like that but I don't know if these are the same ones." And the Polish guy who was frying the bacon said, "Let me see them." I showed them the pouch I had and he dumped them right into the hot bacon grease. The whole pouch of mushrooms and I said, "Hay, they aren't washed yet." And he mumbled, "What's a little dirt more or less." They had mushrooms and bacon to eat. I had brought them a lot of mushrooms.

We gave a job to an old Frenchman. He would help us clean chickens. After he was finished cleaning I saw him taking off and he had a bag over his shoulder, about half a bushel of something. So I said, "What are you taking off with?" He showed me. In stead of cutting the tips of the chicken wings off, he would chop the whole wing off. He had a whole dog-gone bushel of wings. He said, "You guys got enough. We don't have anything." So I let him go. He didn't have any teeth anyway.

We had a nice place to sleep, two stories and double beds, one on top of another. There was this guy; I don't know what rank he was because he didn't have his chevrons on. He was kind of heavy set GI and quite an operator. He had two-gallon cans by his bed. Someone had planted lettuce and greens along the way and he would pick them and make salad in one of those cans. Then he would go into the kitchen and get a steak, (not in my kitchen). He wouldn't go to the mess hall to eat but fry up the steak himself and eat the salad. He would buy up all our cigarettes. We would get a carton of cigarettes once in a while and he would give us twenty dollars for a carton of cigarettes. When he had enough he would pack it all up in barracks bags and he could always get a jeep someplace, and he would take off in the jeep to the black market. He probably peddled them for forty dollars. Doubled his money on it. Like I said, he was an operator who was always goofing off someplace. The other can he used for a pee can for the night. Myself and Pola, a friend of mine, would switch those cans for him and then we would watch what would happen. And he would look at them and smell them and say, "Golly, I don't know which is which." He'd have to use them.

I remember there was one girl came up there, a WAC. She was hanging around and he'd try to make a date with her. "Don't go eating at the mess hall. I'll get some steaks and got salad here. We will have our own meal." He pulled out a bottle of wine. He always had wine or whisky. And she said, "Soldier, what's your name?" And she wrote him up. She was there to see that everything was running right. He walked right into it. I don't know what happened to him.

How They Poisoned It, I Don't Know

I had the keys for everything and one Saturday a semi truck came in. It was loaded with ice cream for Sunday dinner. Well that evening four other guys and myself were going to sample some of that ice cream. Me, would make it five guys. We took our cups and spoons and I unlocked the truck and we went in there and sampled all the ice cream we wanted. We took it out there and were sitting and eating. We sampled all the ice cream and filled up on it and it was great! But then I started getting sick. Sick like I never was in my life. Man I'd vomit and go the other two and I thought I would die. There was a first aide station there so I made my way there to see if they could help me somehow.

When I got there three of the other guys there also and their faces were green. And one guy was laying down on the corner of the floor there and he was saying, "I went through this whole war and now I'm going to die from eating ice cream." And we all felt like that and the medic asked, "How many of you are there?" and I said, "Five all together." He said, "We'll wait until the fifth comes in and then we'll take you all to the hospital." So sure enough, here comes the other guy holding his belly. So they loaded us all into the ambulance and took us to the hospital and I remember going to the door and grabbing for the door knob and that's all I remember. I passed right out; a dead duck. I found myself on the floor. I don't think any of us died but I'm sure that if they served that ice cream to the battalion that there would be some deaths from eating that stuff. How they poisoned it I don't know. But we got back and I thought they would give us heck for eating their ice cream but they didn't. They didn't say nothing. They just let it go.

After a while they got someone else to take over the kitchen and they put me on as a guard on the docks. These merchant marine ships would be coming in and tying up and they wanted somebody to guard these ships. Naturally it would be me. I was guarding through the whole darn war. I guess they put me there for one reason or another. I wasn't the only one. They had a pick up truck and would drop us off along the docks, other guards too. We'd head to the gang plank, get into one of those ships and head to the kitchen. Man they had a dandy kitchen. The ships were run by guys about 14 or 15years old. That's how old they looked like to me. Young kids and they were so capable. There were no more big guys left in the United States so they had to run these ships and they did a good job. Any way, they had everything on the ship. They had fresh eggs and milk and anything you wanted. And they had more then enough. They gave us, maybe 10 halves of pigs. And we would take them down to our kitchen and make steaks. Otherwise the boys said they would throw the food over board so they wouldn't be shortened next time. If they came back, they explained, with some food left over then they wouldn't give them so much next time. And that's how they operated. Which was a dirty thing to do but we enjoyed our pork.

Everybody was Counting Their Stripes

So everybody was counting their stripes. You got one for every 6 months you put in. So many strips and you could go home sooner. That's how they decided who was going to go first. I was with a group waiting for a ship to come in to take us home. We would be sitting around there playing cards waiting, day after day. Finally one day they called us out. The officers were there and we stood at attention. We didn't know what was up. And this officer said, "We haven't received any news. Do any of you boys know what's going on?" This one boy said, "Yeah, there is a liberty ship coming and it's going to be here tomorrow afternoon and that's the ship that's going to take us back home." The officer said, "Tomorrow afternoon!! I bet you fifty bucks it won't be here." The boy said, "I'll take you up on it. Anyone else want to bet?"

I don't know how these guys would know. Toilet rumors and they would know it before the officers would know it. And sure enough the ship came. And it was so over loaded. They had these bunks one on top of the other that were like hammocks and you had to squeeze in sideways to get in. It was so over loaded and all over the whole ship, everyone was gambling. Everyone got paid. Most everyone even got back pay too. So we were waiting for the ship to load up, whatever it had to do to take off. Well, I laid there and the air was foul with all the dirty socks and unwashed bodies. I laid there until I finally figured the ship was far enough out into the ocean to where there would be some fresh air. I made my way up to the deck. I was getting sea sick already and I was looking and we were still tied up. We hadn't even moved yet.

To make a long story short, before we went home, they wanted to first send us to Japan and checked us out to see if we were capable for one more fight yet. One more war in Japan. My blood pressure was up. It was 200. Everyone's was up and some over 200. The young doctor was very suspicious and thought we were taking something to make it so high. "What did you guys do?" he asked. "How do you make your blood pressure high like that?" I said, "You go to the front line and yours will be high too." So anyway, the atomic bomb kyboshed that part of it. As bad as it was I guess it had to be done. The Japanese were a stubborn bunch.

So we were on our way back home on this liberty ship. They would have two meals a day and it was a mess. There were too many people on it plus ship would bob bob like a cork and there would be food all over the floor. We would walk on the spillage it and it began to smell. The whole thing would nauseate me. So I would get an orange and go back to my bunk. And then of course they put me on guard duty. At night the lights would be on inside the ship and everyone would be playing cards and laughing and they gave me a riffle and slammed the door in my face and I would be on the deck all alone. Blacker then night; couldn't see a hand in front of my face. The ship was running without lights. And even up where the captain was, way up top, I couldn't see nothing. And there I was, guarding the ship for eight hours and then when day light would start coming at 8 o'clock in the morning, I was suppose to be finished. But when the time would approach the hands of the clock would jump back to 7 o'clock. And there I was. I had to work another hour! Nine hours before I could go get some shut eye. And that's the way it was going. The time change would cause the clock to jump back an hour on my shift.

I remember I was down at on the bottom of this ship with my back up against the wall and as the waves would come by it would rattle my back rest. We were watching a movie and oh, I wanted to see the end of it but they kept calling me, "Report for guard duty. Novak, report for guard duty." I would wait a little bit longer and the voice would get more commanding. So finally I had to go and I never did finish that movie. Someday I will.

So pretty soon, about 9 days later, I guess we saw the statue of Library on a kind of island. We got off and got on a barge. We came in on a barge. The deportation and others were coming in on barges and they were all yellow. Their faces were yellow. Those that were in the Pacific fighting the Japanese had to take medication for whatever it was they had on the islands and it turned their faces yellow. We could tell where they came from. So finally they shipped us here and there and we came to the deportation station there. They gave us a chance to take a shower. Before that, when we first landed on the main land, they had a dinner for us. It was a dandy: steak as big as your plate and fresh milk on the table, whole bottles of it on the table. We could have as much fresh milk you wanted and fresh lettuce the green kind you can dip into sour cream and eat it. It would crunch and hooo, man, was that good. So I couldn't wait until next day and I went up there again but they said, "No. You can only get one meal like that. You can have some hash." We were back to the same old grind again.

When we got to the last station they gave you a *ruptured duck*. It was a badge to hang around your neck or to hook on to your shirt. It looked like a ruptured duck. That's why we called it that. It meant that you were all done. And then they paid us off. All the time we kept changing the money from French francs to British pounds and then from British pounds to American dollars. Finally, they gave us a bag that we put around our neck with our wallet in it and a bucket for our cloths. We then could take a shower. While I was dressing and putting on my cloths, they started calling me and I didn't take my wallet out of the basket. And when I found out it was missing, I ran back there and they wouldn't give it back to me. They just gave me a hard time story. They continued to call, "Hurry up, hurry up." And so I had to leave it. I couldn't follow up and get my money back. So they robed me at the last.

Anyway that was it. I grabbed a train and a cab and whatever bus and another cab in Grand Rapids and found Sophie where she lived upstairs. It was in the middle of the night and I had an awful time waking her up. She's a good hard sleeper. Finally we were home again to start up where we left off two and a half years ago.

Harmonica playing, "Home Sweet Home."

So I went back to the factory where I was making wings for the airplanes. They had to hire me. The boss was a big man like Baker and he said, "Don't work here. You can find something else." And I was thinking how nice it would be to work on a place where there was a floor and a roof and you wouldn't get rained out. I figured I would really have it made, you know. So I started in and they put me on presses. You had to put out so many pieces. You know how that works, to make top wage. Otherwise they cut your wage. And when you get that many pieces out and get it organized where you can get 300 pieces an hour then they'll raise it to 350 an hour. You can never make top wages.

Arnold (my brother in-law) was working there a long time. I guess they were paying him top wages and also his brother. And the brother was making car tops for pick-ups. I was his helper. We would form that shape of the car top. But they were using steel that was brought in for something else. It was too hard and would crack. The corner would crack. We would grease the corner and it would still crack. So we called the boss over. There we had about 15 car tops that were bad and two were good. And the boss, Sours, looked at it and he thought the two good ones were bad and the other ones were good. He said, "Aaaa, that's not so bad. Keep on going." The brother was a mad Pollock and so he said, "To heck with him. We'll keep on a'goen." So he kept clinking them out and they would all be cracking. We had really a big pile by the time the job was over for the night. I don't know what they did to him.

Ruptured Duck

Anyway I got a different job there. It was making the whole top for the car. There were 4 of us and each one of us would have to press a button for each corner of this big press. The first press would come down and clip the excess metal off and then you would slip it to the next machine and that would form it a little bit. The next one would form it a little more. I had left to go to the toilet I guess. The three of them were running it and I don't know who the 4th guy was. There had to be 4 guys. And that thing hit and formed a dish and then it stuck to the top die and the die went up and they didn't recognize this or realize what was going on. I don't know why. I wasn't there. They then slipped another piece of metal in there and they clomped it down with two pieces of metal. They wedged the two dies together so tight that when the press lifted up it tore this die. The die went up and the bolts and clamps were flying all over and no way could they pry the two dies apart. They had to take them and put them on a freight train and haul them someplace where they could put heat on it to separate those two things. So that was two things that happened while I was there.

The third one was, they put me on a little press and it had a harness. You put your hands in this harness and when a blade came down the harness would jerk your hands back. The only thing is that when you changed stock or something you sometimes forgot to put the harness back on. I was working that press for only part of the day and then the boss took me back to a big one. Arnold came over to the small press to see how I was doing and there was a hand laying there. And he thought it was mine. And boy, I saw him walking around and his face was gray like chalk and all of a sudden he saw me. "Are you all right? Are you alright!" I said, "Yeah. Why?" And he told me about that hand laying there. Apparently the very next guy they put in there forgot the harness and it cut his hand off. So it was a dangerous place to work.

But the worst thing of all was they kept increasing the speed and it got to where it would hurt my heart. One day I couldn't finish the day, it was hurting so hard. I went over to the first aid station and she had me lay down on the couch for the rest of the day and I quit! I didn't want nothing to do with that darn mess.

The Family Goes Cherry Picking

So then I took Sophie and the two kids, Barbara and Franny and we went cherry picking in Traverse City. Ben Gearing's place where dad used to take us when we were kids and Mrs. Gearing was still there. She was very glad that we came. She had to furnish everything for the migrant Mexican families and we had our own tent and everything. The Mexican kids would play around the ladders where we were picking and one time when we were there a ladder fell down on a kid's head. All these Mexicans were carrying this kid and crying. They carried her to the house and Mrs. Geaing got in the car and hauled the child to the doctor. The child came back with her head wrapped. Her skull was cracked but the doctor wrapped it up and she played again with the other kids. When Sophie and I went to town we bought her a big box of chocolates and gave it to her and it cheered her up a bit. She was only about 7 years old. But boy they are tough kids.

We earned pretty good money picking cherries. Sophie and I were picking. Barbara was just a baby, crawling around. Sometimes at night she would crawl out of the tent and we would have to go chase her down. Franny would watch her in the car and we would drive the car into the orchard. Mrs. Gearing would let us drive the car right to where we were picking. And when Barbara would wake up then Franny would blow the horn and mother would come and feed the kids. I just wanted to try it out to see if we could make a living with our hands. And that gave me a lot of encouragement.

So then we got back I continued working on the house. I got it into pretty good shape. It was difficult because I couldn't get water. There were five well drillers there trying to get water. When I bought it no body told me about that, of course. At that time you didn't have to pay the well driller unless he produced. Finally an old grandpa came up there and found some. We pumped it for one day and then it went dry. Then his son came up and he had a big well-drill that he would drill for irrigation for people. He said, "When I get time I will come over and drill you a well." And when he came back he just kept on drilling going right down to the bed rock. 280 feet. And he hit porous lime stone and he drilled into that about 20 feet and there was water. It was quiet a ways down into the pipe and he said that if he drilled another 10 feet he would be through the lime stone and then the water would come clear to the top of the pipe. But, it would be fresh water or it could be salt water. He couldn't guarantee it. I asked him what would happen if it was salt water and he said that he could drive a cedar fence post in there and then I would still have the same water. I was glad to get water. It was limey but I figured it would clear up as I kept pumping. So that's the way we left it. I had built a garage there and we had finished off the house on the inside. We used a kind of a jack and a motor to run the pump. We didn't have to pump by hand. I put a counter weight on the pump and I poured it myself. There was a guy who wanted to buy that place awfully hard but I liked the place. It had two acres and it was prime land right near the golf course and the Grames experimental station.

Truck Mechanic

So when we come back from Traverse City, I went to that place where you pay a dollar to get you a job and I asked him to get me a job for a dollar. He said, "You've been in the army?" I said, "Yeah." He said, "Why don't you go to school and learn a trade?" I asked, "Do they do that?" He said, "Yeah. You can go for two and a half years if you've been in the army two and a half years." Man, I never heard of that. I asked what is available and he said, "Newspaper printing or truck mechanic." So I went over to see the printing place. There was a guy showing me around. He was an old man and his hands were shaking and he was saying, "Oh, this is a good place. I worked here for 20 years." I looked at him and thought, am I going to look like that in 20 years? So I went looking for the other place and there was a guy by the name of Rudy. He was a solider. He had been a car mechanic in the army. In the motor pool. They had just built a truck garage, Alberta Shook on Plainfield. They didn't get started yet so this guy; he was the boss, and myself started it. He was a great guy to work for. He knew a lot of stuff. So he and I opened up the place. And then I started going to school and the government paid half of my wages. Then gradually they only paid a quarter of the wages and finally I was earning my own money.

I liked mechanic work. I fell into it good. I was a good mechanic. I went by the book and I knew a lot of things that the old mechanics didn't know. So that made me feel pretty good. I remember the first truck, a 6 wheeler, I put breaks on it. When I finished I was so proud. Rudy walked around the thing and looked at it and there was a little clip laying there that goes on the break bands. And he said, "Did you put a new one on or is this one you forgot?" I said, "Golly, I don't know." He said, "Take them wheels off. All of them until you make sure." So he made me take all 6 wheels off that darn truck. As it was, all the clips were on and I don't know where that darn clip came from. That taught me a good lesson. From then on I was sure when I did something._

So I looked this one truck over when I had it on a hoist. I talked with the truck owner and said, "You know, this would be a good time to trade this truck in. It still looks good but there were several broken leaves in the spring and the tires aren't that hot. Why don't you trade it in now?" He went over and talked with the boss, Albert Keller and Albert sold him a new truck and it was because of me talking him into it.

Tape 7, Side A

Allan Keller was quite a salesman. One time a guy came in there with a pickup and he locked his keys inside the pickup and so he went to Keller, there, Keller was running the joint. He was the big shot there. He had some trucks on the road himself. He said, "You left your keys in the car and your windows are all locked. Don't worry about that," he says. "Our men will take care of that. Walt, go and unlock the pickup." Oh, boy, there I was! I didn't dare to argue. I had to do it. The only hole I know of into the cab was if you crawled underneath the truck there was a cap under the floorboards. It was covering the break fluid container there. So I took a screw driver and poked the cover off and I could see the door knob through the crack. I took, naturally, a couple coat hangers, wired them together and stuck them through this crack underneath there and hooked the door. Hooked the handle and opened it. So from then on I had the coat hanger hooked on the tool board. It became one of our tools for opening up the doors.

We had a good job there and saved up a little money as we went along. Usually we had one check for utilities and one check for food and clothing and one check we had left over and filed it way. That's how we saved up a little money. Sophie was caning a lot of food from our big garden there. I had a big garden but I couldn't cultivate it. So you know what I did? I went over to the neighbors and asked if I could borrow his horse and cultivator. And he said, "Yes". I was surprised. I never would have loaned my horse to anyone. But he did. It was a nice gentle horse. He pulled the cultivator and I cultivated the whole thing. I would stop once in a while to take the horse in the shade for a rest and a drink of water. He worked for me real good.

We had a bunch of chickens and I would go to the back of the store and all through winter they would have some green lettuce and cabbage and stuff like that. I would chop it up for the chickens and they would lay all winter. They wouldn't realize it was winter time because they were getting green stuff so they would lay. In spring we were going to get a few more because we were thinning them out as we needed fried chicken. So I bought a box full of little chickens. We took them upstairs and fixed them up a place there. And wouldn't you know, one of them fell between the two by fours right down to the very bottom. This is inside of the wall and it lived!

It got hungry and started peeping and it was right next to our table. And we couldn't eat. That little thing was hungry and was peeping and I was thinking maybe I could get a bucket of sand and dump it in there and smother it or something. But I really didn't want to. So I took a cover from a jar and made a sling with heavy thread. I then put some chicken feed in there and lowered it way down in there to the chick. I had a flash light and I would flash my light on it. He stood on the edge of this Mason jar cover and was eating. He was so engrossed with eating that I was able to pull him all the way to the top and I saved him. I felt like quite a hero. Anyway I was glad to get him out of there.

Bought a Farm

So that is how it was. After a while I got to thinking it would be nice to work for myself. My brother Jim had a farm near

Luther that was near where our homestead was. My dad had a place near there. Jim seemed to be doing good on his farm. He had some cows and a few pigs and a little farm tractor. Oh, man, I wanted some of that. So I started looking around for a farm. And maybe about 20 miles from his place near Hersey, Michigan, I found a farm that looked pretty good. It had a beautiful house. It had been made in Detroit and reassembled. It was made out of heavy maple. Everything was maple. The windows were carved nice. The barn was good timber. The farm was 160 acres with 10 acres of maple grove and this whole thing he wanted $12,000 dollars. And I bargained him down to $9,000 and some hundred dollars. And that's what I bought it for.

I looked it over first and there was some good land and some was real bad, almost blow-sand about 3 acres of it. The rest of it was fair. And so I figured in Michigan you can't expect anything better. There will be good land and bad land on 160 acres. So I bought it and hoped Sophie would appreciate that house. One day I told Alberta Shook I was leaving and Ruddy, he asked Mr. Keller, "Do you think Walt can make a living on a farm?" Mr. Keller said, "Yeah, he's going to do all right." So that's what we did.

It was very early spring, lots of snow. Snow up to my knees and butt and we got to the house. It had one of those big furnaces down below with lots of pipes. You old timers remember that. It had an opening with a big grate on top. The grate let the heat out into the middle of the house. It had a heating coil for hot water in it. And there was a half a ton of coal there yet. Apparently he was firing it so it wouldn't freeze after he left. That would have been Mr. Reeves. He was a World War I veteran so I could get along with him pretty good.

So there we were. It was hard to get started. I got measles, then mumps one right after the other. I don't know why, I never got those sicknesses as a kid but now got them. I may have been run down. I wouldn't have been surprised. It was difficult to get wood. Sometimes I would see a wooden gate. They used poles for the gate and I would steal those poles and cut them up for wood. I would pray over it to have my neighbor please forgive me and I'm sure he would. He knew I was in tough shape. His name was Leland Loker.

All my neighbors were real good neighbors but some of them took advantage of us and turned their cows into our good wheat fields. They were careless about their fences and then their cattle would get into my corn. One day I locked up a cow and wouldn't give it back to the guy. He was an old timer and had all his sons living there with him. Oh how he wanted his cow back but I said, "No! I'm not giving your cow back until you promise to keep him off my place. All your cows, keep them off my place." Finally he promised. Oh, it was just like driving nails into him. But he did promise and he took his cow and I never had a problem with him after that. We got along pretty good. Another guy would let his sheep onto my place and holy mackerel those sheep would trim up your place in no time flat. I fired a couple times with a shot gun and drove them out. So we settled that too. The third guy...I had a bunch of corn in shucks. That means corn cobs and all were on the stocks and I didn't have time to get it all from the field. And during the winter when I couldn't get into the corn field this neighbor guy would turn his pigs in to my field and let them go in there and feed on my corn. So outside of that, they were very good neighbors.

So we got a hold of a sow. She was a Durock type and was a 4H registered sow. She had killed all her little piglets so the farmer sold her for meat price and she was already bred back when I bought her. And when she was about to have little ones, I went over to Bracket's lumber mill to get some lumber. I was going to build a crate for her so she couldn't turn around and kill her little ones when they would come but I was too late. She already had her little ones. She was laying there just as happy, grunting away and they were all sucking away. About nine piglets, all uniform. And that was because she was registered and they always give you nice pigs and a lot of them, twice a year.

In time we had 7 or 8 sows, all registered. We were making good money on those little pigs. Sophie over here, she had an incident where she felt sorry for the little pigs so she turned them all out into the corn field. The corn had been harvested but there was still a lot of corn around. 50 pigs in that corn field! And I came home and she told me about this and I thought, "Holy mackerel! How am I going to catch them 50 pigs in a corn field?" But she wasn't excited about it. She went out and with her magic she called them and out they came. Just like birds coming out of the corn field. And they followed her at a trot back to their mothers. So then she turned the mothers loose too… 7 big sows weighing about 400 pounds. How am I going to get those things back into the pens? I said, "You got them out. You get them in." I thought I'd teach her. But no. She started walking ahead of these pigs and calling them and they followed her. She didn't even drive them. They followed her back to the pens and then they jumped in.

At another time, I came into the pen area and this one pig reared up against the partition that kept her in. I could see the partition was giving way, so I started shoving against the partition to keep it from breaking down. Sophie saw what was going on and wanted to help so she rammed her shoulder against my back to help me. The pig was trying to bite my chest but she couldn't get her teeth into my chest because I was wearing a leather jacket but now with Sophie helping and I couldn't get away. I had Sophie on one side and the pig on the other. I was caught in-between!

But Sophie made up for it. We had loose pens where the cows could freely wander in and out. (We weren't milking now anymore.) We also had a pen full of piglets. A guy told me that when I go to town to bring him one. We were going to town that afternoon, so I reached down into the pen and picked up a piglet by the hind legs. That thing began to squeal! The squeal attracted a cow that came to its aid. The cow that had been standing around now charged in to help this squealing pig. I began backing up. I threw the piglet at the charging cow but the cow didn't care. She came at me and knocked me over backward on the straw and was going to gouge me with her horns. And here comes Sophie from behind me with a pitch-fork in her hands. I don't know where she come from. I thought she was in the house. She jabbed that cow in the face several times before the cow finally let me go. It was one of the things we had with cattle. They are gentle as can be but something like a squealing piglet can upset them.

We had a bull by the name of Flash. We raised him ourselves. He was a nice quiet animal. Well, once in a while, my brother-in-law Arnold would come from the city to the farm with his whole family: Arnold, his wife Stephanie and the kids Arnie, Suzie, Patsy, and Michelle. The kids always wanted to see the cattle and this time Arnold and myself went along with the kids. As we were all approaching the barn, I could see the bull's head sticking out around the corner and when he saw us coming he lowered his head and come out of the barn like a race horse. I didn't know an animal could travel that fast and he was coming right for us with his horns protruding. The kids ran to Arnold and he grabbed them all and was holding them. His jaw dropped open. I knew I had to do something. I didn't know if I had to rustle that bull or what. But I stepped forward so I would be between Arnold and the kids and I yelled his name, "Flash!" That raging bull whorled right around and went back into the barn. That was close. We didn't have Flash much longer. We eventually sold him. They can be dangerous.

We sold a lot of stock. Almost every week a truck would be there picking up cattle or pigs or something. This time we had too many pigs so I took some in a pick-up to the sale. We had a sale going one day a week, every week in Big Rapids. We had an auctioneer selling our stuff and people from Armors and all over would come to buy stock for meat. So we sold those pigs at a good price and there was a crummy restaurant there for the farmers and buyers and cattlemen so we would go in there and buy ourselves a hamburger and a cup of coffee as a reward for selling the animals. It was kind of a reward. We worked hard and the hamburger and coffee was an extra that we would buy for ourselves and the check would help too, of course.

Barn Fire

As we were going home we noticed smoke coming over the hill. The closer we come the more we realized that it was coming from our house, our place, but we didn't know if it was the house or the barn. We knew it was one of them. Finally we came over the hill and could see it was the barn. I don't know what happened if the pigs knocked the top lights down into the straw and set the pig house on fire and that set the barn on fire or if it was the wiring in the barn that set it afire. I just had it rewired and Jim my brother and I just painted it. We gave the barn two coats of red paint. The barn looked so nice and had new wiring in it. Everything went. All my live stock went. All my pigs burned up; the little ones and big ones, all my equipment, two new milkers, separator and a chopper I bought. I had it in the barn and hadn't even used it yet. It had a new belt. All the hay, all the grain in the silo went. The silo burned up but it was so cold at this time of year that the silage that had been frozen stayed frozen. So what we had was a column of frozen silage without a silo. I immediately built a long tough to the silage and let the milk cows could go in there to eat. Lucky the milk cows could go in and out of the barn so they were all saved from the fire. I would feed the silage even before it would thaw out. I had the fattest cows before spring of anybody around there. I didn't have a barn and fixed up a shed for the cows but the cows milked good anyway even thought it was cold. So that's what happened.

We suffered a misfortune. But one of the things was I had borrowed money on the place and I had to carry full insurance so the insurance paid off in full and we were able to rebuild the barn. We built it <u>real</u> good. We had our own lumber and plenty of timber. I had Bill cut it up. We made it a Quonset type barn. More then a Quonset more like a Gothic roof on it so it would shed the snow better. We used the very best of roofing on it and secured it to the elm boards and when they dry the boards are just like iron. So that barn should last for years and years to come and we did a good job. And we built a pig house and kept on-a-go'en.

Heading for a Warmer Climate

Finally, the snow got cold and the winters got cold and Sophie wanted to try out living someplace better. A little warmer. She had low blood pressure so the cold affected her harder then anybody. So we had a sale. It was a good sale. I made a few thousand on it. But of course the prices went up a year or two right after the sale. But I guess that's normal or just my luck. In 5 years the farm sold for 3 times the price. So we took off to California. We fixed up a trailer. I make a top on it like a covered wagon and it had a tail gate that could be let down and we used it for a table to do our cooking.

We had a new Rambler but it didn't have air conditioning and they were telling me about going through the desert and Tina was just a baby and I needed that air conditioner. I figured I needed it. I didn't know what I was to encounter. So it cost me $400.00 (the price of two cows) to get one in there. And you know, we never even used it. We went through the desert and never even knew we went through it. It was hot though one time. I remember the baby Tina got a nose bleed. We pulled up under a tree. As we were pulling under the tree there were three other cars going for the shade but I got there first.

There was a rustic old store and we went in there and an old grandma was running it. She was sleeping in her rocker behind the counter. I asked for some ice for Tina. She didn't have any ice so she sold us some popsicles and we used these popsicles to stem Tina's nose bleed.

Fresno, California

So we didn't have any real incidence going up there (to California). We stopped at George's house. Our brother George was a body-man there, an excellent body man. Bootsey was his wife and they had 3 girls and 2 boys. And she could cook, aaa, man, she could cook. She's cook turkey, biscuits and gravy and everything. So we were enjoying our stay. It was 112 degrees when we got there but it was so dry you couldn't feel the heat. You could feel it but it was bearable. You could work outside. I was hoeing Bootsey's rose garden and I didn't realize it. She asked, "Do you know how hot it is?" I said, "No." She said, "112 degrees."

So Barbara and I decided to take a walk through town to get acquainted and to get accustomed to this temperature that we were suppose to live in. I had a Strep throat. I use to get it every once in a while. I don't get it anymore. I use to get it if I worked close to the dirt, like planting trees. That's what we did with the farm of ours. I told you the 3 acres that were sandy. We planted it into Christmas trees and they sold us red pine. But then when the Christmas trees were ready for sale they wouldn't buy them. They said, "No no! Scotch pine is what you should have." Every time I would listen to the Government advisors they would screw me up. They sold me the red pine in the first place and then they wouldn't buy them. So Sophie and I grew a forest of red pine. And I mean it is a forest right now, about 60 years ago.

We had to eventually find a place for ourselves. They were telling us about the coast and how beautiful it was so we drove over to the coast and it was a sand storm blowing. Oh, my, gosh, it was pitting the windshield. It was already dark. I found some type of scraggly motel and rented it and we got in there. We struck towels under the door to keep the sand from blowing in. When it was nice and sunny and the weather was good it was an ideal place but no body realizes what was in store. So we got out of there as fast as we could, back to Fresno we went. But I didn't want to impose on George and Bootsey any more so I rented a place at $400.00 a month. It was high then. We started looking around for a house to buy. When Bootsey found out we were living there and didn't come back to her house she gave us the dickens. But I know we had to be a somewhat drag. We didn't want to impose on them any more then we did.

Snakes and Scoprions

I was looking in the paper and there was a 2 1/2 acres of ground and a house for something like $5,000. I went to look at it and it was the junkest place you ever saw in your life. The 2 12 acres was part of a 5 acre piece. The house was the one the homesteader built there years ago. The house didn't have any 2X4s just boards running up and down and batting over the cracks and then they put plaster board on the inside but if you wanted to hang a picture, the nail would come out the other side. The wall was only about an inch and a half thick. But it had a nice kitchen and it looked like a porch made into a kitchen. It had windows all the way across the front of it and it had a white brick chimney in back of the stove and the trouble was, there was a man living in there. And every time we'd come in we'd find a lock on the door.

He must have been feeding chickens. There were chickens around there. He was watering them, we could see that but we could never catch him to home. I could see that he was hiding someplace so I decided to-heck-with-that and the next time we came I brought a hack saw and I sawed that lock off and threw it away and Sophie and I carried everything that was in that house and carried it into the barn. There was a shaky old barn there. I guess the roof was alright. Nothing wrong with the roof. And pigeons all around that place! I had to take a shotgun and blast away at them. And once I killed a few of them, they didn't come back no more. But the neighbors hollered at me for shooting at them but I couldn't live with them things.

What we did is we scrubbed everything with Lysol. We scrubbed the floors, walls, ceilings, everything. We washed everything down and sprayed it off with a garden hose and when everything was dry we got some cheap paint. Inside paint isn't expensive. We painted the whole thing, ceilings and all and got some new linoleum and put it in there and it looked pretty good. We washed the windows and pretty soon I heard the man rapping on the window and I opened the window. I don't know why he didn't go to the door. I guess he was scared. And he was mad.

He said, "What did you do with my gold? My gold?" "I don't know about your dang gold. If there was any it would still be in those dressers we hauled over there to the barn." So he was satisfied. Apparently his gold was still there. But he kept hollering to me that he was a squatter and he had squatter's rights and I had no right to kick him out like that. And he had a lot of Indian artifacts there. Apparently he had been walking a lot through the hills and mountains there picking up that stuff. He had some of those rocks that the Indians would grind grain with. A hollow rock with another rock that fitted into the hole. And he had several of those things. I think what he was also doing was spraying barns with lime. Farmers use to do that and instead of money he would take whatever the farmers would give him in junk. He had 50 gallon barrels of paint and car motors and truck motors and I just can't imagine. The whole 2 ½ acres was like a junk yard. I told him, "If you don't get this stuff out of here…," I said, "I'll give you a week to clear it all out but if you don't get it out I'm going to charge you rent for a month." He had lived there for a month. I said, "I'll charge you rent for a month." And he took it seriously. He had some buddies and they had a truck and they all worked like beavers and he took every bit of that stuff out. It was valuable to him. He had a place to sell it.

And another thing he pulled a "smart one". He knew the people that had owned the place and he had somehow got a permit. There was a garage with a board nailed across the door and it was all cobwebs in there. You could see a little and in there were all cowboy saddles, chaps, lariats, harnesses, victrolas and everything they had during that time. I guess they put it in there and closed it up. All that stuff was probably 30 or 40 years old. And he went in here with a little hand rake and went through all that stuff. I guess he did pretty good.

Grass around there had been growing and piling up on the land for so many years that it was like walking on a mattress. Of course there were snakes and scorpions and all sorts of stuff in here. I didn't want Tina to get stung. Those spiders had that emblem on their stomachs. They were deadly things. There was lot of them spiders around there. So I got a permit to burn and I burned that stuff but I could just burn the top and the rest of it was damp. A few days later the grass would dry out and I would burn it again. I kept burning it and burning it until I got close to the soil. I bought a disk and would disk it . I would rake it all up and drag it, level it all off. I had a bulldozer come and dig a hole. This chicken coop had grapes all over it. They were the green grapes for wine and they were as long as from my elbows to my fingers, big bunches of grapes like that. About 15 pounds in a bunch. They were all over that chicken coop hanging there. The barn was there and tree roots had grown and lifted one end of the barn up.

So I kept burning those buildings, the chicken coops and that barn. Except the garage. There was lots of lumber there so I reinforced the garage to make it into a good tool shed. In fact, I built a shower in there but if there was any wet ground then the mosquitoes would come. It was hard to take a shower because the mosquitoes would eat you up. And the trees, aaa man, they were all overgrown. And the grapes would grow way to the tops of the trees. This was like a garden. The 5 acres had provided a living for the farmer and his family. He had a mule and made rows real close together for green crops. During apricot season the farmer would hire help to pick them and then they would cut them in half and put them on a little rail road and a cave. He would put the cut apricots on the little flat rail cars and put them into the cave. He had smoke in there and the smoke would cause the sugar to come to the top. They would bring in good money with that. The apricots were the sweetest I had ever eaten. The apricots would turn transparent when left to ripen on the tree. Folks around there would have fruit stands that time of year and people from town would come driving by and they would buy all we had. We had a box and ants had gotten in there but the people didn't care they bought them anyway. They were so good.

We had some black figs that were the size of a pear. They looked like a pear. They would hang down and be full of sugar. It was so overgrown that I would walk on those limbs. It was just like a floor. I trimmed the trees all up and took out all the bad trees and kept putting them in that hole and kept burning them. They let me do that as long as I had a permit.

I put into a college as a boiler operator because I had been working doing that at a college back home. They said they didn't have a boiler operator job and the only thing they had open was a janitor job. The operator job would be open in a short time so I put in for it and hoped I could get my foot in there. And then I went and got a job at a car wash. We would be wiping these cars as they would be coming off the line. A big black guy was on one side of the car and me on the other. He had big hands and would take a Turkish towel in either hand and go swat, swat, swat. He's get his half of the car dried and then he would get some of my half because I was too slow. I had to jump into the car and drive it away before the other car would bump into it. They were all different makes of cars. Some were floor shifts and some had shifts on the steering wheel.

Man, I had to get them out of there and I didn't care what gear I had them in. I would give them enough power to get them out. So I worked there but it was so hot I couldn't eat. Lucky there was a hot dog stand and sold the foot long hotdogs and root beer. So that is what I would eat. I would order one of the footlongs and sit there in the shade and drink my root beer. And this guy he owned this place and said, "You don't look like a poor guy. I think you have some money. I'd like to sell you half interest in this place." I knew it was making money but he had two boys that were working there and you couldn't tell them kids anything. Well, they knew quite a lot on their own but...they also knew their father owned it. So even though I was suppose to be managing it they wouldn't listen to me. So I didn't want to get into anything like that and eventually they called me into that college.

Tape 7, Side B

Harmonica playing

So I was called to the college and quite my car wash job and started in over there. They didn't have anything open as a boiler operator so I took this janitorial job.

Just Over the Top of the Clouds

The winter months came to Fresno and it started clouding. Clouds started to come. We would get ice on the window but it wouldn't snow. The mountains would be snow, where it was high up. And all that snow on the mountains, when it melted was caught in a reservoir. The reservoir was a huge thing with walls that looked like a freeway. Cement way up there. The water was caught and then used all summer. There were ditches above the ground. The ditches all had sluice gates. Mine did and you could pull it up every two weeks and flood your whole place for 24 hours. That would soak the ground up and then it would be good for a couple weeks and then you could do it again. There was always water in them ditches coming from that mountain. Like I said, it was overcast. No sun all winter long except if you wanted sun you could go up the mountain and get way up there on the top above the clouds and there would be kids skiing and sliding and just enjoying the sunshine. We'd go up there for a weekend. You'd be up so high that the airplanes would be flying below you. Just over the top of the clouds. So that's how it was up there. It was a strange country.

It Looks to Me Like Nitro!

I don't know if I told you about the old man that was living there on my place. He left that garage and some stuff in there that was good like a hydraulic jack and a few things that I could use. But then it was junked up with a lot of bottles. I bet those bottles may have been valuable and it never downed on me. So I backed the trailer up there that was in the back of the house. It was hard to get at. I would throw the bottles on the trailer. Then I heard the voice behind me, "I wouldn't take that." I was about to take a bottle that was hung on a wall. It was wrapped up in a thong, a leather thong. There was some yellow liquid in there. And he says, "It looks like nitro to me." Aw man, I heard that so I called the police and they said they'll send somebody over there and so here comes a cowboy: a tall guy with yellow cowboy boots and a cowboy hat.

He looks at it and said, "It's nitro all right and it's old and really charged by now. Concentrated now." I said, "What would have happened if I would have thrown it on the trailer?" He said, "There would have been just a big hole over here." Boy it was that close. So that old timer did me a favor by appearing there just in time as I was about to pick up that nitro. This guy in yellow carefully took that bottle and carefully carried it to the farthest corner of my property and he dug three holes there and he deposited that stuff in there. He told me not to plow there for three years. It was dangerous stuff.

What they used that stuff for was to crack the sea bottom which consisted of about a foot of top soil over the top. The rest of it was the consistency of red brick maybe a bit less hard. You could drive a sharp pick into it. That was about all you could do. But what they would do was if they wanted to plant a row of fruit trees, they would dig holes for these fruit trees then they would dab a little cotton into the nitro and stuff it into the hole where they wanted to grow a tree and then they would detonate the whole thing and it would crack that sea bottom. And then the roots and water could penetrate it. And that's what was necessary to farm that area.

Dug his Hind Claws into my Stomach

Daughters Tina and Barbara were living with us yet. Franny was going to college already back in Michigan and New York, different places. So they picked all the apricots and olives. We had lots of olives, some along side of the road and on our place too. There were two kinds. There were some big ones that looked like plums and some small ones. So Sophie and the kids would pick them and they would take them down to the factory and they would give them a check for them. They would either give them olive oil or a check.

Well this time the kids sold apricots and Barbara brought herself some clothes and Tina wanted a rabbit real bad. She found one, a white one with black ears, a big one. So she bought it. I had to build a house for it. She would tie a string around its neck and lead it around and play with it. She was on the farthest end of the yard when Mother hollered, "Dinner." I went out and knew that rabbit would take a long time to get home so I just picked it up and put it over my shoulder like you would carry a baby. I figured the rabbit would appreciate me carrying him but he didn't. He dug his hind claws into my stomach and he almost gutted me, he was that powerful. There I was without a shirt, (like I am now) and some people think that rabbits are so naive and gentle but boy that one wasn't. He fixed me good.

Tina for some reason she liked angle worms and after the watering the worms would come up to the top of the ground and she would pick them and put them in a candy sack she had. She would carry them in her pocket. One time, we went across the road to visit our neighbors. They were interesting people. The lady herself would make artifacts that looked like a bottle inserted into a piece of wood, She would take a bottle and cover it with mottling clay and scratch it with a fork and insert pieces of tubing in the scratches there to look like branches. Then she would spray it. You would swear it was a hollowed out piece of wood, it would look so natural. She would have a whole table of that stuff and she had a place where the women would gather and sell this stuff and that's how she would make her money. So we went up there and she noticed that bag in Tina's pocket and she took it out. She needed glasses so she held that bag right up to her face to see the "candy." "What kind of candy you got?" She saw those angle worms and she let out a scream. Tina had to pick up the bag.

So I made Tina boat to play in because Barbara wasn't home very often anymore to play with her. There was a little house there too and Sophie fixed it up real nice for the kids to play in it. But I made this boat and I gave her a fish pole with a magnet on the end. She would pick up nails. I bent them into a shape that she couldn't hurt herself. She would collect the nails at the end of the fishing pole. She would spend a lot of time there. Then she would have a saw horse to play on too.

One day she was out in the grass and she come back and said she found a watermelon. I didn't know what it was so I went with her and there in the grass was a watermelon. Oh, my, it was over two feet long! And fully ripe. I had to take a wagon to bring it into the house. I don't know how it grew in the grass. Surely if I cut the grass out and work up the ground it would grow twice as good. So I worked on it and made me a watermelon patch. Planted a lot of watermelon and you know...I never got a single watermelon out of there. You had to know how to farm that land.

I started telling about the picnics we put on for George's kids. (George, my younger brother. Sophie and I would have peanut hunts and things like that but this time it was a mystery thing. And we took and hid a treasure and then we drew a treasure map for them to follow. It would lead them to a tree or rock and there would be some more instructions and from there you would go someplace else. It would go on and on. It took Sophie and me about an hour and a half to two hours to lay that thing out. Finally we came back toward the house with this treasure map and we eventually came behind the house and there we buried this treasure for them. So then we invited George and family over, his in-laws came, and the boys. When we gave them the map, they took off on a run and it was no time at all before they made that whole circuit. I think we underestimated them and should have made it a little harder. It didn't take them any time to get back to the original beginning where the treasure was hid.

We'd make a rope pull. We'd put a rope over a mud puddle and then choose up sides and get as even a group as we could and Sophie and I would be engineering this thing. The kids were having fun: neighbor kids and George's kids. As they started tugging on this rope, the women looking through the window saw the action and they would come out running. They couldn't resist it. They grabbed hold of that rope. Then George and all the men folks came charging out for the other side, so we had a lot of fun. Quite a pull.

Where I was working there at the college, there was a guy working there by the name of Perry. He was a black man and he and I would get along real good. We would eat our lunch together and talk. He would tell me all the things that were bothering him. He was telling me about a plot of land that was willed to him in Louisiana. And he said he would like to see it. I said, "Well, what's stopping you. You have a car and it's not that long of a drive." He said, 'I can't ever see it." I asked, "Why?" He said, "I have to go through Texas and if I go into Texas, why, I can't get gas unless I tell the people, "Sir." I have to "Sir" to them." He said, "I was here among you guys for so long, I hate to go back to that era when we had to say "Sir" to everybody." I kind of laughed I didn't understand really what he was talking about.

Wedding in Louisiana

But there was a wedding in Louisiana. Fran was getting ready to get married and they invited us over. So I decided instead of driving we would take a bus and let someone else do the driving and to just enjoy the ride. And back in Michigan when you would take a Greyhound, you would ride kind of in luxury. But here it was the darnest contraption. It was like riding in a truck in a kitchen chair in the back, like that. No comfort at all, hard riding thing. But one of the things…when we would get toward the end of the day or toward dinner time they would stop at a station. A bus station and they would have dinner there. It was really a good meal. One you could really sink your teeth into. There would be fried potatoes, baked ham and vegetable and desert. All you had to do was to take your plate and walk through there, take what you wanted and then take care of the bill. So we were looking forward to these meals.

Finally we got to Texas. The state this boy had been telling me about. I don't know how I got mixed in. Apparently there were a bunch of blacks in the back of the bus. I guess they were in the back…I don't know. But as the bus stopped and people started heading for the lunch counter, I got mixed in with the black people. I noticed the driver of the bus was pointing to me but I didn't know what he wanted. So I went into this room. It was a nice clean room but there was no furniture in there, just a bench all around the wall. These people sat down on this bench; so I sat down on that bench and I waited to see what was going to happen. There was a window there and then I guess at a signal, they all got up and stood before this window in a line. I was standing in line too. Then I could see that they called out their order and they would pass them a plate and then they could sit down and eat. One of the guys told me to go around and go with the other white people. I guess they didn't want any trouble. So I went around to eat with the other people where they could help themselves. So I could see what this Perry was talking about then. They were really isolated. The black people didn't want any trouble so they didn't want me butting in on them.

Perry's Perfect Yard

Well anyway, this Perry was having troubles all the time and he would tell me about it. One of the things, he would be carrying water to his car by the buckets. I asked him, "What's the matter?" He said, "I got a hole in the radiator." I said, "How did you do that?" He said, "I set the radiator cap on the radiator and it fell off and the fan drove it through the radiator." I said, "That's tough." He said, "Naw, that's alright. I'm going to get another car pretty soon. A company come along and they are going to refinance me and buy me a car and pay off all my doubts and everything." So he came back with a Plymouth. It was quite similar, the same vintage as the car he had. And a few days later he was caring water to this car again. And he says, "You know...same thing happened to this one. I put the radiator cap there and it fell off and went right through the radiator." So he was right back where he started from except now this company would take his check and they would give him a little money back to live on.

He had quite a family too. He was married to, I think a Spanish lady. He had 2 or 3 kids, daughters about 15 or 16 years old. He said, "I'm going to move out. I got a place where the white people are living." I said, "How come?" He said, "I can't raise girls in a black neighborhood. They get pregnant." "And", he says, "no one is going to be able to say that I'm junking up the place because it will be the nicest place in that area." And he lived up to his word. He would plant trees and flowers and he kept that yard just perfect.

One day I was at his house and went in and saw their furniture was boxes, orange crates and stuff life that. They didn't have any decent furniture but the place was spotless. Real clean. He was trying to live up to the standard of the community the best he could.

Perry, he was talking with me one night and a guy come up and talked with us a while, a white man. He was working there with us too. Then when he went away, Perry said to me, "Did you notice how prejudice he was?" I said, "No. I didn't see anything prejudice about it. He talked to you and me both about the same length of time." "Oh," he said. "He was really prejudice." I'm surprised. They see something there that we don't see.

Anyway, some of this junk that was around my place was a trailer. It was a big box type trailer for a semi. It was made out of angle iron with 2X4s bolted in these angle irons. It was an old timer of some sort. I didn't know how to get rid of that thing. It was something that they left there. So I figured I would burn it up. I started a little fire and the inside of the 2X4 caught on fire. Can you imagine that? It would glow like a hot coal. I seen that at night. I thought the fire was already out. I don't know why I built that fire. It may have burned some of that trailer up. These 2X4s would start burning and everyone burnt off. When they burnt off, then all that iron fall down into a pile. I had a heap of iron laying there in the morning. I never seen it happen like that before. The wood must have been treated with something. Something that soaked into the wood.

But anyway old Perry…he was a window washer, by the way, he wouldn't do janitorial work. He would wash windows. And once in a while he would get a hold of his whole check before the sharks got it. If he got a hold of his whole check he would go to town and stay there until the whole check was spent. He would do that about once a year. But then he would loose his job. So he had a system for that too. He had lots of kids and he would take his wife and kids and some neighbor kids, I don't know. And he would go to the office and tell them, "Either you guys give me back my job or I'm going on welfare with the whole kabuttle." And they didn't want that either so they would always give him his job back. So then he would go back to washing windows again. Nobody would bother him washing those windows. He done a pretty good job, I guess. Anyway he wanted to do better so he hunted around someplace and found a truck.

He said, "I'm going to go into junking business." He found someone that would buy iron. So I told him, "Come on over to my place and I'll give you some iron." "Good" he said. "I'll haul it over there and sell it for half." So he came with that truck. I was curious. We loaded up that truck with all that iron that was laying around there plus any spare iron. We had quite a load. We started out with that thing but the battery conked out. But there was a place we could pick up a used battery not too far away. I got him this battery and some gasoline and we were hauling this iron. Finally we came to this place that bought iron. It was quiet a ways away but they paid more for it then any place else. But the only way they would pay the full amount is if it was cut into 2 foot pieces. We didn't have any means to cut it into pieces. So he had to sell it for what he could get out of it. I think he got about $5.60 or something. He was going to give me $2.00 but I couldn't take it from him. So he went out of junking business. It didn't pay out very well.

Mexicans Who do More

We were having a lot to do with the Mexicans. They are really good people once you get acquainted with them, they accept you and they know your not deviating but are square with them. So then, they were having a money rising. They wanted to start kind of a cursero. It's really a religious retreat and they wanted to build their own retreat house. They were saving money for this retreat house. They were selling different things like tortillas and stuff to raise money. The women would usually do it but once a year they would have a carnival. They would take over the whole park. They would have all kinds of things there. One of the things was a "pit barbeque" they called it. The meat was cooked under ground. They'd have a hard-wood fire going. I don't know how they did it. The meat was wrapped in, oh, about the size of a loaf of bread, a whole bunch of these pieces. The meat itself was wrapped in herbs. It was so tantalizing that if you walked by and smelled it you had to buy it. You couldn't resist it. And tender, just as tender as can be, the meat was so flavorfull!! They really knew how to do it. They cooked it all night to get it just right. That was one of the good things they had.

Boots and Brother George

So Sophie and I got George's kids over there. Well, one of them and his friend. I don't know how old they were, maybe 8 or 9 like that, two of them. It was going to be quite late so they were going to be staying over night with us. First thing they did was to start trapping my chickens. They got a box and put a stick under there and some corn. They'd tie a string to the stick and hide behind some bushes and when the chicken would come to eat the corn, they'd pull that stick out and trap my chickens. I heard them things squawking so I put a stop to that.

We dressed the kids up like a couple hoboes. Colored their faces and gave them a little skit. They learned it pretty good. So we put that little show on. They won $5.00 for putting on the skit. So the night they were staying with us a neighbor come over and he was saying they had a swimming pool party and these two kids were throwing rocks into the water. I said, "It couldn't be our kids." So he said, "There are a couple kids like that down the road. I'm going to go tell them off. I'll tell their dad." I guess he went and accused the other kids but our kids weren't coming in. It was already getting late and I didn't know where the heck they were. So I said, "Let's just turn the lights out and make believe we're sleeping and lets see if they come." And sure enough here they come sneaking in. So I cornered them and asked them, "Did you throw rocks into that guy's swimming pool?" They said, "Yeah." I said. "Well, you better come along with me and apologize then." So I took them down there and knocked on the door. I woke the guy up and told him. I said, "I'm sorry I said I thought it wasn't our kids but it was. They got something to say." They apologized and he said, "Oh, boy, now I have to go to the neighbors and apologize to the neighbor boys." So that was incident number two. The chickens and the rocks.

Well, I was cleaning up next day around the park and collecting all the money. They had me as a treasurer from different booths. So I told my wife to take the car and the kids and go home and I would come home later. Well, I got home and a fire was going. The whole back field was a blaze. I asked them kids, "What happened?" They says, "Well, we were sitting up there and there was some kind of guy and he was smoking and he caught it on fire." "Are you sure you weren't smoking?" They finally admitted it. So I took them home. A couple days later I saw their mother Boots and said, "Your boys earned $5.00 on the skit." She said, "Yeah, but I couldn't let them have it." I says, "Why not?" She says, "Well, when they got home they chopped up the neighbor's water hose. I had to buy them another water hose." And I had been wondering why George had built a large board fence around his back yard. But it didn't hold. They opened it up anyway. He had a lively bunch there.

He had 2 big trees there by his drive way. He thought what a good idea it would be to make an arch way. They were fur trees and real tall. So him and his neighbor took some rope and they pulled these trees down and wired them together and made an arch out of them. They were nice for about a week but for some reason the branches started to grow straight up. It was a terrible thing, sticking up there.

Well, Bootsey called me one morning, "George come in here and dumped a whole bunch of fish in to this freezer of mine and they are looking at me." These fish you catch in the ocean are down so deep that when they come to the top their eyes pop out. He had been fishing and brought all them fish in. Instead of filleting them out, he just dumped them into the freezer. She went to get some food and the fish were look'en at her and she didn't like it. And she said, "If you want fish, come and get em or else I'm going to throw them all out." So I had to come and get them, there were quiet a lot. About half a bushel of fish. I took them home and fillet them out and I only had a little bit of fish. That's what he was complaining about, "every time they filet out my fish I end up with a little sack full." He said, "I want to bring all the fish in. The whole fish." So that's what he did. Bootsey put a veto on that very quickly. It wasn't as bad as the moose head though. He got a bargain somewheres. So to surprise her he brought this moose head in. I don't know if he nailed it to the wall yet or she saw it before he nailed it.

I know he had a boat there when we where there. The boat was all in pieces. He had all the pieces. Of course he was a body man and maybe he could put it together again. At least he figured he could. It was some bargain.

Harmonica playing

Jack was a lonely cowboy, with a heart so brave and true.

He learned to love a maiden, with eyes of heavens' own blue.

They learned to love each other, and they named their wedding day.

When a quarrel come between them, and jack he rode away.

He joined a band of cowboys and tried to forget her name.

But on the lonely prairie she waits for him the same.

> Your sweet heart waits for Jack.
> Your sweetheart waits for you.

Out on the lonely prairie, where the skies are always blue.

[Ted Tupish taught me that]

Jack left the camp next morning, we heard his sweetheart's name.

He said, "I'll ask forgiveness. For I know I'm the blame."

But when he reached the prairie, he found a new made mound.

And his friends sadly told him, they laid his loved one down.

They said when she was dying, she grieved her sweetheart's name.

And told them then to tell him, to tell him when he came.

> Your sweetheart waits for you Jack.
> Your sweetheart waits for you.

Out on the lonely prairie, where the skies are always blue.

Lonely and slow Harmonica playing

So that's about all I got. Sorry about this noisy tape I have. I don't know what's the matter with this duplicator I got. It's so noisy. I'm afraid I'm spoiling these tapes. But anyway...

Tape 8, Side A

Back to Michigan

One day, Sophie said, "If you want to go back to Michigan it will be all right with me." At work they had sort of promised me a boiler operator job but now they said, "When you come back you can have the job." I said, "If you give me the job I won't go." But they said, "No." Anyway, I figured Sophie missed her family, so we put the house up for sale. I had just finished building Tina a house up in a tree. Each time our buyer would come to look at the place his kids would make for the tree house. I think they got him to buy it. So we made about four thousand on it. We had a big yard sale and gave away the couch and lamps to the church. We were getting rid of everything we couldn't fit on our trailer. When at last Sophie sold a box of boxes, I thought we were all set. Then a truck came with a washing machine we had won on some long forgotten ticket. I told the Mexicans to go raffle it off again.

The next morning real early we heard music. The Mexicans called that "Mananeta" or "farewell" I guess. Their priest came too. We had donuts and coffee. One of the ladies asked how long would we be on the road. I said, "seven days." She said she would pray for us for seven days. I was reminded of this when a dear crossed the median in front of our car. He couldn't make it across so in his confusion he turned around and came back at us. Just as the car was about to hit him, he jumped and I saw his white belly over my windshield. We heard the scratch of his hoofs on the roof. Some how he made it clean over the car. He had hail and snow but made the trip fine.

We stopped into Ted's when we got back to Big Rapids. He said for us to stay here with him until we got situated. So we had a nice visit that day and the next morning I went out to see if I could find a place to live and over by that church in Reed City they were having a summer festival. Father Cusack and Father Gallagher were there. Cusack was the priest that instigated me going to the corcero. So he gave me a hug when he seen me, a typical greeting at that time and Gallagher too. And there in Reed City was a Chevrolet garage and I went to see if I could get a job as a mechanic there. Usually I would work as a mechanic, off and on. I did that in California too. The guy at the Chevrolet garage had also been at the church and he said you must be really into those priests. They gave you a hug. He never saw anything like that before so he gave me a job right off the bat like that. So then I had to kind of relearn about Chevrolet cars and started working for him then.

So then I started looking for a house and there was a lady and she rented me a couple rooms. She also had a barn that had rooms with all kinds of stoves and beds and things in there. She helped me furnish our rooms. So that afternoon I went home to pick up my family and told Ted, I got a job working at Chevrolet as a mechanic. I got a house too but we have to move the beds in yet. So I came back to Ted's to pick up Sophie and the kids. He was surprised that before the day was over I had a job and a house already. Some of the people he's helped would sponge off him for a month or two. But I was lucky.

Maintenance Man for Ferris State College

So I was working there and put in an application at Ferris again, the college, as a boiler operator. It wasn't very long before they called me and John Miller the chief engineer said, we got operators for the boilers but I could use an all-around guy to maintain the place. So I was a maintenance man there for the last years that I worked there.

I did take a boiler operating ICS course. It took me about two years to master it but then when they learned I was a certified boiler operator then I started getting a lot of breaks and also a raise in wage. So now I started studying air conditioning and heating all thorough these buildings. I would take the books and blue prints to the bottom of the basement. It was someplace that no one ever used. It had a light and was silent like a tomb and I could study real good in there. So I learned all the blueprints on the machines and I could correct the things that were eating up the electricity and fuel, like the air conditioner, on the science building.

The science building had three big lecture halls and they would be air conditioned 24 hours a day, whether they needed it or not. There would be 3 days off on weekends and other days longer and sometimes it would be cool and still all the air conditioning would be chugging along for the whole building. I asked them why and they said, we have animals in there. There was one room with rats in there. So they would air condition the whole building just for this one room. I had them put in a window unit and I would shut the whole big contraption off. One motor would use $7.00 of electricity an hour. We had big motors there. Maybe pumps would be running and they also had safety pumps so that if one pump broke down they could switch to the other one but they would be running both of them for no reason. Things like that, I was able to correct and save them enormous amounts of money on utilities. So again they would give me a raise on that because I done pretty good.

I had previously put in 3 years working at the Fresno College. After I came back, Ferris College paid the difference in the 3 years toward my retirement and with the time I had actually put in to Ferris, I had almost full retirement. So I put in for retirement at 62 years which gave me a little break there.

Cottage on Muskegon River

We wanted a place of our own so Sophie, Tina, Barbara and I went driving around looking for our future home and there on the Muskegon River, about 4 miles from Big Rapids, was a cottage. It had been built for fishing. It was on a 150 foot lot and was right on the river. It had a nice dock and was made out of ceramic block. It had one big room and had a lower level that opened almost right out onto the river. And we bought that. The kids and wife agreed but it had nothing, not even stairs, only little cubby holes for sleeping. So I backed a trailer up, I saved the 2X4 and took everything out. Made a clean sweep. We were sleeping in the basement in the meantime. I then put a sub floor in and tar paper and masonry floor and then I drew the rooms out on the floor with chalk the way I wanted them: the bathroom, two bedrooms, kitchen and we rebuilt that thing from scratch. We made a real nice cottage out of it. Where the porch was we added stairs to it and included it in the main house and then I bought 3 or 4 lots across the road. One lot we used for a garden for many years there.

Canoeing

I had a canoe. Sophie called it "Pea Pod." And we used that extensively. We had a great time. Tina and I would take that canoe out sometimes and just let it drift and watch the wild life. There would be all kinds of things hidden. Gophers would be chattering above your head. They wouldn't be freighted of a canoe.

One time there was an inlet there and we let the canoe drift into this inlet and there was this robin bird and he was bathing. He was just splashing water all over himself and having a great time. And he didn't notice there was a cat sneaking up on him. She was ready to pounce on that bird and then the bird saw our canoe and he flew away and that cat turned on us and fire was coming out of her eyes and if she could have jumped onto the canoe she would have tore us apart. Her dinner had taken off.

And at night, toward evening the frogs would start crooking in the bayous there by the big lake we were on. And one would start corking first, crook, crook, then another one would start in, crook, crook and then a third one, crook, crook, crook, until the whole caboodle would be crooking away. And then they would just shut off, just like a snap of your fingers and everything would be quiet and then the bull frog would start in again. Tina was so taken by them she said, I'm going to go get a blanket and I'm going to sleep here. She wanted to be with the frogs for the night.

Searching for Warm Climate Again

Well, as it would happen, inevitably, the kids kept growing up one by one and taking off on their own. It wasn't long before Sophie and I were batch'en again by ourselves and Tina was in college. Tina was the last one to leave home and so then Sophie wanted to get away from the winters. She had low blood pressure and the winters were hard on her. Anyway she bore up real good while she was in Michigan. We were going to take a little trip. I had been different places while in the war and Stark, Florida was a nice little town. And Tyler, Texas was a really nice town.

Both had possibilities but this time when we drove into these towns they had grown. They weren't nice little towns anymore. They were overgrown metropolis. Anyway, we went all across the United States. We went to Texas. We went to Florida. We went to California again. We checked everything over and then when we come back, I asked Sophie where would you like to live? And she said, lets do the trip all over again and then we can decide. I said, No. We cannot do that. Florida is the closest about 1,300 miles.

So when winters come we would drive to Ocala, Florida. They had a nice rec hall where we learned to clog and line dance and put on shows there. Stage shows about twice a month with lip singing and so on. I got me a guitar there. We were doing that for a number of years and eventually we wanted to stay all the time. So we had an auction sale. We sold the place and every single thing we had on the place even a pile of rocks we had there. Sophie's sister came and bought them. She still has them. Sophie had been collecting these rocks from all over wherever we went so they were quite unique. But her sister's got them now herself.

Second Life

We bought a place in Zephyrhills, about 70 miles south of Ocala. It's a nice little town and there's Bet mar Park. My brother Ted and his wife had a place there once and they liked to swim especially Dorothy his wife. They instigated a swimming pool so we got a nice swimming pool here. They moved out of here to Tennessee but my sister Ann (Nelly) and her husband Joe Cherry live here. So we have family here now and are pumping along with my sister Ann and her husband.

So just recently we had a hurricane Charlie come. It looked like it would come through our camp and these houses are not built for storms. They usually get flattened out. Ann was going to stay at a school here that opened up but I don't like crowded conditions so I packed everything in the car and headed out East out of the path of this hurricane. We stopped at a town called Kissimmee about 90 miles from here to the east. This hurricane was supposed to come along the west coast. I figured 90 miles aught to be pretty good. So we bedded down in this motel and what do you know, that hurricane followed us. It started on the west coast and went to the east coast right where we had escaped. So we threw some pillows and some comforters into the bathroom there and we got in there and held the door until the rattling stopped and the hurricane passed us. It was really glorious because I expected our house to be flattened but when we got back everything was the same. Thank God.

Well, that's about the end of my narration. And what comes from now on is in God's hands.

Let me tell you about a dream I had. It was back when we were in Ocala yet. In the little trailer we had two couches that made up into beds facing each other so we each slept on our own little couch there. And I was dreaming that I was about 17 years old and working on the farm. It was a general farm and had some real nice Guernsey cows and they and stanchions and everything was in order. Each cow had a record posted at its stanchion, under glass. These two boys and myself just finished chores. The older one was scraping the barn. He had a little tractor, like a mower only it had a blade. The other boy was probably my age or a year or two older. He had a disinfecting can, a spray can and he was disinfecting the stalls and I had a rag in my pocket and he would motion with his head for me to wipe the glass that held the records. He would spray them a little bit and then I would wipe them clean. It was early in the morning.

The arrangement that I had with the boss was that I wouldn't receive any pay because the boys didn't receive any money and he didn't want me to flounce it around. So he said that when I'd be leaving then he would give me all the money and if I needed anything like overalls, shirt, shoes then he would buy it and keep a record of it. So that was ok with me.

I had been working there now several months and I figured I had enough to buy myself a modal A Ford. They didn't cost very much at that time, maybe $40 or $50 dollars and you could get a good one. And I already had that much money saved up so things looked very bright for me.

The food there was very excellent. They'd have fried potatoes, pancakes, ham and bacon and coffee, a good breakfast and then after breakfast we'd be sent out to do different work there on the farm, whatever needed to be done.

Well, this morning I was done with my cleaning before the boys finished putting their stuff away and I walked outside. There was kind of a stone wall on one side of the barn yard and the sun was shining there and the chickens were scratching around there for worms. I could hear some younger kids and they were messing around in the hay mound. The barn door was open there. I didn't want to go to the house myself so I was lingering around, kind of waiting for the boys to finish up then we would all walk in together.

Then something said to me, "This isn't true. It is a dream." I said, "Dream? This isn't true? If I am not I then who am I?" It was that clear of a dream that I couldn't believe that it was a dream. I felt like I do now that I am I and if anyone would tell me that this (now) is a dream, it would baffle me. Well it baffled me then but then almost immediately, I believe, I woke up and there I was laying in this bed 70 some years old. All my options gone already. I felt down. Oh, no…all my savings and stuff, I couldn't collect. I don't know what or why I had that dream but when they tell us that we are going to live again, I can see how possible it can be from that dream. It was so real.

The other dream I had was, we were already coming to Florida for the winter, and I belong to the veterans of foreign wars for quite a while there and we would sell poppies. You probably remember them. The money would go to the hospitals and homes for the veterans to cheer them up a little bit and whatever needs they might have we would help them out in that way. The captain of this unit that I was in his name was Heartline and his wife, the women were in it too. And I had a dream this night that I was on a tarmac and there was an airplane setting there. It just had one motor but it was a huge job and I was looking at it. I was on the outside looking at it and a door slid open with a clang and two guys with those pilot hats walked out and the door clanged behind them unlike an airplane door. Then there was one window but there was a blanket over the window so I couldn't look inside. I was standing some distance from this plane but the side of it looked kind of jaggedly and old. I could see inside and there was a woman standing there and she had a veil on and a long brown dress and there was nothing in the plane except I saw the woman in there. And that's all! Then I woke up and didn't know what the heck it meant or anything but my neighbor was also a vet and he came over and he said that this Heartline and his wife were jailed. They were in jail in Reed

City. And the clanging of the door, I recall because I use to bring communion to the people in jail and it was that same "clang" and I knew the airplane referred to a jail. And this guy told me about these people being in jail.

I felt that I had to go and see them so I drove over there and I was wondering about bail. The sheriff and deputy came out to see what I wanted. The sheriff was a real hard man but I asked what about bail for these people and he stuck out his hand and said, "you put $3,000 dollars in cash right into my hand right here and I'll let them go." What the heck is going on here? Then he went away. And he wouldn't let me see them. No, he let me see the man and I asked him about the bail and he said, "No. They can't hold me over 30 days and then they got to let me go." He was sweating it out. The woman they wouldn't let me see her at all. Then so I went back home to Big Rapids and went to the Big Rapids jail and I thought I could find something out. I talked to the jail keeper there and he was human, more human. He told me that if I had given him that money I would never have seen a penny of it again. He said they would consider that as belonging to the incarcerated person and that she would have to pay the judges fees and the lawyer's fees and all the jailers' fees and there wouldn't be anything left. I didn't know that that is how it worked. That is what he told me.

So then I was going to see the lawyer that was representing these two people and I went to see him but he wouldn't talk. He didn't want to talk about cases pending like that. Then I went home and I was looking through my trunk. I have all kinds of stuff in there. I don't know what I was looking for but a piece of paper fell out and it was that paper of recommendation from the banker from when I was borrowing money for the pigs. And the name on it was the same as the lawyers.

So when I inquired, I found out the recommendation was from the lawyer's dad. So I had a carbon copy made and mailed it to this lawyer and so the next time I seen him, he acknowledged me. And he told me the reason they were jailed was they were drawing unemployment and that they were getting money and they didn't record this money and what this money was, when they would help with a bingo game every body that would be out there helping would receive $10.00 and they didn't report the $10.00. It seems like they were $3,000 behind. She was. It didn't say anything about him and the lawyer said that if you can come up with the $3,000 it would go a long way to get her out of jail. She had a hearing and had to pay everything up and so when I got home I went to my bedroom and prayed to the Lord.

We were just getting ready to go south for the winter and I asked, am I just making all this up or is this dream really true and you want me to do something about it? So I asked the Lord am I making this up or is this revelation and He said, "Do you think that you could go to Florida and enjoy yourself there for the winter knowing that somebody is languishing here in jail and you could have done something about it and you didn't?" And that is the message that came to me. So I didn't have any choice. I wrote out a check. It was to the state and gave it to the lawyer. And while we were here in Florida, she wrote a letter thanking me for it. Apparently they let her out. She asked me how she could repay me. I said, well, (I knew they didn't have any money) I said, the money I have comes from the Lord in the first place so if He wants you to repay somebody He will let you know. And that's all I said. I heard later, from other people, that they were doing well. She had gone to school and he had a steady job and it seemed like things were going good for them. And praise the Lord for that.

And when I was thinking, why was I chosen? One of the things, I had $3,000 available to me and another thing, I use to bring Holy Communion to sick people and old people through out the area around Big Rapids there and one of the people that I was bringing communion to was the wife's father of this judge that was hearing the case. I was bringing communion to the judge's father-in-law. This judge was a hard nut and would always give everyone the hardest sentence he could give. And I tried to talk to him on the phone but he wouldn't talk to me about the case so I wrote him a letter and I explained to him about the good things about this family.

I told him about how one time it was snowing and raining and we were trying to sell these poppies. It was too cold for me and I was going to quite but this Heartline said to me, "Give them to me and I will sell them." And he stood there in the freezing rain and snow and he sold them poppies and I wrote that in the letter to the judge. And I am sure that he read it. So in that since I had these facts and that recommendation to that lawyer and I knew the judge through bringing communion to his house to where his father-in-law lived. So the father-in-law died there in the house. So that is how it was with this other dream that I had.

So this other case, it wasn't a dream. Our sister Ann and her husband Joe and Sophie and I would go to a dance over here not too far away, to the Lion's club. And of course, we would ride with them in the back seat. And I never would buckle my seat belt. As I remember we never had these buckles and I looked at it as a nuisance. I figured in the back seat I would be safe anyway. So I didn't bother with it but this one night when we were getting ready to go home, something told me, "Buckle up. If you don't and are in a car wreck, you will fly into the front seat." And not only It told me to buckle up It told me what would happen if I didn't buckle up. And so I didn't hesitate. I buckled up and then within maybe 5 or 10 minuets the car was totaled out.

We were going up a hill and there was a cross road there and a white truck was going to go across the road. He didn't see us coming and he drove right in front of Joe, maybe 12 or 15 feet, that close, he zipped in front of us. And there was nothing Joe could do. He's an excellent driver. We were watching it too. It was like a white sheet was draped over your windshield. And we hit that truck and the hood come flying toward us and came flying through the windshield. The only thing that saved us, or we would have had our heads cut off by that thing, was the truck's drive shaft, the rear wheel drive shaft. When we hit that shaft, the car could only go under the truck so far. I thought the glass would cut up my sister's face and Joe's face but we all got out and there wasn't a scratch on us except where we had lunged into those harnesses. It was black and blue where the straps held us back. And Joe's shoes didn't have any soles. It tore the soles off his shoes, the impact was so great. So that was again that voice.

This one time we were living by the river yet and Tina was living with us and her and her girlfriend wanted to go to the show. I don't know who took them down there but I was suppose to come pick them up when the movie was finished at a certain time. Well, when I went up there they weren't there anymore. I talked with the manager there and he said, yeah, they were here but they took off with a couple guys. There I was sweating it out. I couldn't find them so I came home. I walked up and down the road in the moonlight and there was a rock there by the stream. I sat on the rock and again the Lord spoke to me, "He says, "don't you trust me?" I said, "My gall! Do you know where they are? And are you going to take care of them?" And He said, "Don't you trust me?" And those words lifted me up. I came home then and called the girls home and she had a brother that was kind of retarded, a young guy. He had some sort of beat up old car. I got him on the phone and I told him the situation. And he says, "I think I know where they are." And he took off in that thing and he found the girls someplace and he brought them back home. And "Don't you trust me?" I trusted Him and everything turned out good.

So then that young guy would come walking by sometimes and it would be freezing and he didn't have any coat or sweater so I would take him to the house and fix him up with some cloths. Then I gave him some money so he would trim my apple trees. He was suppose to be working as a trimmer on a farm. And I would help him out any way I could. He didn't know what was going on but he done me such a great favor that I could never do enough for him.

So that is what I was doing there at that time. I was distributing communion and helping the priest any way I could but also I would go driving around the country and visited different people that couldn't come to church because they were ill or old. I drove quiet a way, up to Hersey on those bad roads. There was a farmer, oh, there was a beautiful farm. Every thing was all painted up and it had some nice cattle, feeders. He was always raising some birds, turkeys, chickens, doves and he was very busy and he kind of resented his wife being sick because he would have to tend to her. But I would bring communion to both of them. Sometimes he would take off on me. I would have to catch up to him.

One time I caught him and I told him I come all the way over here and you can take a few minuets off to receive the Body and Blood of Jesus. And so he would stop for a while. He wasn't always too enthused to see me but his wife received the lord and would pray sometimes. She was getting more and more sick and along the road would be sweetpeas and vetch and they were so pretty that I would pick a bouquet of them for her. She would have the farmer get a glass by her bed there. She kept getting worse and worse and finally she couldn't swallow the host so I would have a little vile of the wine, the blood of Jesus and I would give her a few drops on her tongue. One time I come up there and she looked like she was about gone, so I just started singing. I was singing a hymn and I heard a follow up, like an echo and I looked and she was singing with me and her voice was coming and she was enjoying this.

Well, finally, I come up there and there was a bunch of cars around there and I went in. I could see her bed was empty and I knew what happened. So I sat down and the farmer come in and they were all going to leave so he could receive communion and I said, "No. You guys all stay here and we are going to pray for her." And we did that. We had a little prayer meeting there. They said they had taken her to the hospital and when they came to pay their last respects, she sat up with them and they brought all the family pictures and they all reviewed the pictures they had taken. Then she passed away. So then the farmer told me not to bring him anymore communion. I told that to the priest and he said, "Well, visit him anyway." I guess I did and I took my wife along and he was in the barn sitting among his pigeons. All kinds of pigeons, all kinds of buildings full of pigeons. They were laying eggs and were sitting on nests and there were pigeons everywhere. We never interfered with him farming after that. Somebody told me later that he sold the farm out.

Tape 8, Side B

May he keep you whether you are near or far away.
May you find the long awaited, golden day today.
May you walk with sunlight shining, a bluebird in every tree.
May there be a silver lining, back of every cloud you see.
May your dreams bring you sweet tomorrow, never mind what might have been.
May the good lord bless and keep you,
Until we meet again.

Yeah, this one place was, I think was run by a German lady. It was out in the country. It was a home for the old people and it was a dandy place. I had to drive a long ways but I would go out there. Especially this one time and the bridges and roads were washed out and I had to drive miles out of my way to get there. The people lived upstairs and they had one room where I would meet with them there. All the Catholic people would come and the Protestant people would come too. And we would have a regular prayer meeting there. Of course, the Protestants wouldn't receive the host but they would receive the blessings anyway. So they would get to telling stories when they were kids and how they would sneak out the window and go to the pasture and ride the horses like I use to do. One woman told how she got down, she said she would slide down the horses neck while the horse was grazing. It was quite a trick. I never thought of anything like that. I don't think my horse would put up with it. But stuff you would hear there, it would really make my day. This one time I was going to go upstairs and the house mother or owner, why, she just set down on the stairs and she wanted to share and she told me all her problems and we prayed over them. So that was really an interesting place. They had a garden and planted sweet corn for caning and everyone would be sitting around outside pealing off the skins this sweet corn and snapping beans and also peas. They were always busy. I think it was a nice place to live out there in the country where you could work in the garden if you wanted to. That was one.

Another one was a farmer and he was alone in the house. His daughter, that he was living with, would have to go to work and she would leave him there. They would lock the house and sometimes he couldn't unlock it and I would go around the house looking for a way to get in there. He was in a wheelchair and tried to unlock that thing. But once we got together we had a real good visit because he was a farmer. I'd tell him about the Polish horse my brother bought. My brother didn't know it was a Polish horse. The horse didn't understand, they didn't understand each other. So he thought the horse was balky and he went out and told the people, "You sold me a horse that doesn't respond." They said, "Do you talk to him in Polish?" He said, "No." "Well you have a Polish horse and you have to talk to him in Polish." Well, Jim knew enough Polish that he could say what he needed the horse to do and the horse did obey him. So that horse had to learn another language. But that was funny and that guy really enjoyed that story. We talked a lot about different events and he would receive the body of Christ and we would say a prayer and I would go to another house.

Well there was this other house. It was right in town and a guy by the name of Tomottol lived in it. He lived with a woman and she told me they had no relations, no sexual relations at all. I said, "I don't care. It's up to you." She said, "No, we are like brother and sister, because it is cheaper to share one house." They had a big garden there.

He said he couldn't speak English. I don't know if he was lying. If he was I couldn't catch him, no way. He was a spy from Russia and they would send him out to locate different people that they wanted to contact. He said he would disguise himself and prowl around until he located them people he was suppose to find for the Russians. But I could talk to him in Polish and he could understand Polish alright. I kept coming to him and sometimes he would walk off. He was down the road once and I caught up to him with the car and we had service right there on the hood of the car in the middle of the road. Eventually the lady passed away first. He would be there eating an apple with some salt on it. That was his dinner. He was telling me, "Now, the only thing that matters to me is Jesus Christ." So he came a long ways.

He was telling me about Tito in Argentina. He said that was the best government anyone could have. Because he was with the big shots and if he got sick they would send an ambulance and it wouldn't cost him anything. He was saying how the people had to give their crops to the government and they would all share because it was communism. This one guy reserved some potatoes so he could sell them on the black market and somebody squealed on him so he took these potatoes and dumped them in the ocean. Of course they forced the truth out of him the next day and apparently there was a spy watching him because they knew what he did. So they took him out there in the ocean and tied a rope around his neck and gave him a bucket and made him go down to the bottom of the ocean and pick them potatoes and bring them up. They probably killed him anyway in the end. He said that one guy spoke something against the government and they tied him behind some horses and just dragged him to death. His skin wore off. He said that was a real bad thing to do but he then said, "He shouldn't have said anything bad against such a good government." So that was Tomotto.

There was another guy that was real interesting. I was bringing communion in a housing area like a little village. They had the old people pay as much as they could afford. They had a little kitchen and a living room and bedroom. They were real nice places. I was bringing communion to this one guy and as I was leaving I noticed one of the parishioners sweeping the sidewalk there. I said, "Hay, what you are doing over here?" He said, "Well my father-in-law lives here." I said that I might as well bring communion to him too. But he said, "No. He is an atheist and does not believe in God." "Well, I got to see him anyways." I went in there and here this guy was 6 foot something tall and stout and he was all man. He used to be a marine. He would go into the kitchen and fill up a cup with coffee right to the brim and he would bring it in to show me that he could do that without spilling a drop. And he would put it by my side and then go get himself one.

He had some boxes and they were round boxes that were filled with cookies, two different kinds of cookies. He would bring out the box and offered me some and coffee and said, "Now we will talk." And he was lonesome. Very lonesome and everyone and his family were parishioners and his daughter too but they couldn't talk him into accepting the Lord. I would talk to him on that subject and he would have answers for everything. But then when I left I took his hand and said the Lord's Prayer and he said, "You can pray but don't hold my hand." And so that is what I would do every time I visited the guy next door, I would go and talk with him. He would tell me different things like how he had to murder a man when he was in the marines. It was on orders. The guy dug his own grave and he had to shoot him. I think that had something to do with it. He didn't want to face the Lord. I don't know but this one time I was in a hurry for some reason and we talked a little while and I drank my coffee and ate my cookie and I jumped up and was going to start out the door and he was standing there and he looked horrified. I was going to leave and forgot to say the prayer. When I saw what was happening, I sat down, said the prayer and then he was alright. He clamed to be the unbeliever but I think the Lord was coming to him through me. So when we were getting ready to go South, Sophie and I, he was in that home for the terminal and I spoke with him then and I said, "John, I'm going to leave you in the hands of the Lord." And he said, "OK." And he acknowledged it. He said, "OK."

This Tomottol I was telling you about, the Russian spy catcher said that he wanted to go to confession but he couldn't speak English so I told our priest about it because thought he might know a priest that spoke Polish. And he said, no but he said maybe you can be the interpreter, but I felt funny about that because I didn't want to listen to his intimate story, his confession and then relate it to the priest. I said I don't think that would work out. So we left it that way and that's how he died. But I think just because he acknowledged that he wanted to receive the Lord all his sins were forgiven. I think the Lord recognized him that way.

Our priest used to bring communion to the prisoners in our town. And he had to go someplace and told me to bring communion to them. Well I didn't have any idea what this entailed so I went over there and I told the jailer. He said come in. And he clanged that iron gate behind me and that is what I heard on that airplane too. And he locked me in there with the inmates and then he opened the door to a room and those that wanted to receive communion came in there. Well I didn't think everybody would come and I was so surprised to see so many young guys that I knew very well coming in. I said, "What the heck are you guys doing here?" They goofed someplace down the line and were now in jail and all dressed up in the yellow clothes, orange really. And we had a regular meeting down there. I tried to do a little preaching but they would take over and they would do the preaching. They knew the bible as well as I did maybe better. So we had a good meeting.

This one time I come up there and only one black girl come. She wanted to receive communion. I didn't know what to talk to her about. We said some prayers and she received it. At the same time we were having problems with the Knights of Columbus hall. We built it on the promise that we were assured that it wouldn't be taxed but then after 3 or 4 years they wanted all the back taxes. Apparently a new group of politicians took over. Because we didn't have that kind of money they were going to sell the place from under us. I was sharing this with this black girl

and I could see the interest in her eyes and how she took interest.
We had a good visit. I guess He knew her heart.

So I went down to Ludlow faire (Tampa I believe)
Lost my tie I know not where.
And half way home or somewhere near,
Brought quarts and pints of Ludlow beer.
And then the world was not so bad,
And me myself a sterling lad.
And in the lowly mud I laid,
Happy till I woke again.
And when I saw the morning sky,
Hi, ho it was all but a lie.
The world is still the old world yet,
And I am I and my cloths are wet.
There's nothing for me to do but then,
To do it all over again.

There's a gold mine in the sky far away,
And we'll find it you and I some sweet day.
There'll be clover just for you down the line.
We will find it you and I, my pal of mine.
Faraway, faraway, we will find it you and I
Some sweet day.
And we'll sit up there and watch the world go by,
When we find that long lost gold mine in the sky.
Take your time I know your growing lame.
I will measure it in the sky when we find that claim.
And we'll sit up there and watch this world go by,
When we find that long lost gold mine in the sky.
Faraway, faraway, we will find it you and I some sweet day.
And we'll say hello to friends that said good-bye,
When we find that long lost gold mine in the sky.

Sophie and I were taking a walk the other night and we were almost up to Ted's old house that he build here on the corner. We were at the house just before his and it was dark, real dark in there. We heard a terrible noise, a challenging vicious noise. Some kind of a beast. We hurried by and turned around the other way and crossed the bridge and came back home. So next time I decided that next time I would carry a cane with me. Well, I didn't have a cane yet. I was walking by myself and it was early morning and still dark. It was a different street. This was Apache Street and that darn noise come again. And the beast, it had crossed the road in front of me. I would see its tale sticking straight out and it was about the size of a middle size dog. And the noise came from it. I clapped my hands real hard and yelled. I thought it would run but it wouldn't run. It just turned around and waited for me. It was about 10 feet off the road. Its eyes were like fire.

As I walked, it started walking toward me only it was walking on the grass parallel to the road. And we passed each other and I was talking real gently now, "Poor pussy, nice little pussy." I think it was a wild cat. That's what I think it was. It was a male and had a female cat underneath one of the buildings and that darn thing....I never heard a noise like that. It just sent chills down my back. So then after that I would carry a cane. But I don't think a cane would be any weapon against that kind of an animal. So I let the people know at headquarters about it because I didn't want to tangle with something like that. But since then I hadn't seen it. I saw a smaller cat a few times. I think it was a female one. But that big son-of-a-gun had to be a wild cat. Couldn't be anything else. A wolf would have barked and this thing didn't bark just challenged me with all its might and it meant business. I walked backwards so as not to turn my back to it. I think this is what saved me!

Guitar playing
Little Joe the Wrangler

This story-song reminds me of that little guy I use to work with at Baker's riding stable. His son Bud was a cowboy from day one. There was nothing he didn't know about horses.

Second Life

When we were kids our dad would plant either string beans or pickles, on contract. We'd pick them during the summer. It would give us some money for clothes or whatever for winter time. So this company would send out a supervisor to check out the field and see how everything was doing. He would see that they got a good product for sale. He came over one day, a portly looking man, dressed up nice, a real gentleman. We all met him out in the yard, my mother and all us kids. Dad was away somewheres. He had a chain across his vest made of elks tooth or something like that. He had a golden cross. It wasn't very big, maybe an inch and a half maybe two inches. It was a plain cross. My mother was thrilled when she seen that. He said I would give it to you but it's a gift to me but if you give me your address I'll mail you one. And so he did.

I think my mother valued that cross more then anything she possessed as far as jewelry. She had a black velvet dress that looked very nice with that golden cross but it wasn't for that reason but because Jesus was crucified for her that she valued that cross so much. What else about that cross...I was working, we all were adults now and I was working at Fresno, California College. I was a janitor there and there was a Catholic church there right on the street or the street was built around it, I imagine because it was wooden and very old. There was a very old pastor there too. I worked nights so I would stop in there before going to work and say a few prayers. We called it a "visit". Then I would go to work. It would make me feel like I could meet just about any problem. Anyway on the opposite wall there was a picture, a sacred heart picture off to one side, on my right. It had a golden cross just like Mother had on but then the next day the cross would be gone and next day maybe it would be there again. And it would be an on and off thing and I would always look at it and but I never took time out to really examine it.

And then one day, I was sweeping the floor. We had a long corridor to sweep, push broom and I would put an oiled cheese cloth over the broom bristles and it would pick up all the dust and run it across all the way back and forth. But like I said this was night and one of the doors was cracked open and out of the doorway shown a bright light, all the way across the hall way. In this light was this picture of the sacred heart. It was the same size about as the one I saw on the wall over there in church except it was all in gold. And I stood there kind of petrified, scared I guess, not knowing what was going on. Finally it went away and I finished my work. I didn't say anything to anyone. I thought something else was going to happen. Something attracting me but nothing was happening so the next day I stood about where I was before and went into the office and turned on all the lights and cracked the door like it was the night before but I couldn't get that light to shine. It didn't shine at all, only around the doorway. So that's the way it was.

Then one day we went to see our sister Mary in Colorado and they were living for the summer down in the valley and they had a two room little house and a couch there that would open up into a bed. So that's where Sophie and I would sleep and no sooner would I lay down but she would pull up a chair and sit there talking half the night. So I told her about that vision I had and that cross. And she said let me tell you about that cross. I thought this cross was buried with my mother but it wasn't. My older brother had it and he gave it to my sister Mary the youngest sister. She said that she had it for a while and she wanted to give it to her older sister so she had it cleaned and she laid it on the dresser and went to the bathroom for something and she said she came back ready to pack it and it was gone! And she didn't hear nothing. It was just her and the landlady there. She called the landlady and they searched and searched and nothing developed. They couldn't find that thing. So the only thing I can think of is when we see mother again, I think maybe she's wearing it.

Guitar strumming soft n slow

The End

Notes from the Transcriber

A daughter's heart sings if her father asks a favor of her; and more so if the favor is to transcribe his memoirs. I cannot describe the joy and pride I experienced in 2007 when my father asked me to do this task.

When I accepted, he mailed eight, 90-minute, double-sided tapes to me. I immediately popped one into the cassette recorder and smiled at the sound of my father's voice beginning his narration. I soon realized that transcribing from a cassette recorder required numerous pressings of the pause and repeat buttons. I continued my transcribing as I searched for a transcription machine. When I finally found the machine, I found them to be too pricy, but by that time my fingers began to have a rhythm of their own. They typed, pushed pause, typed, play, pause, rewind, type, play and pause. I would listen to a sentence, push the pause button while I typed it and then listened to another sentence. Often I would need to go back and re-listen to the sentence to pick up a missed detail.

Soon it became evident that the transcription process would take longer then I had originally estimated. My father was very patient. He would say, "Don't worry. Take your time." That felt wonderful as I often became lost in his voice and his story and before I realized it, I had forgotten to press the pause button and would have to rewind a considerable amount.

These eight tapes comprise the second half of Father's life. Previously he wrote a book mainly about his younger days and farm life. His first book he had professionally edited and typed. There is a copy in the Big Rapids, Michigan library and I made five other copies.

This current book is more about Father's adult life. I am not a professional editor or transcriber. But even if I were, I would still keep the rhythm of the tapes, the rhythm of the spoken word rather then the edited written word. We speak in sentence fragments, run on sentences, errors in verb usages and exclamations. All of these I have not edited out.

After every half a tape was completed, I would mail it to Father for editing. His patience kept up for a full difficult year.

I completed the transcribing in 2008, the year my Mother, his devoted wife passed on.

During the process, I asked Father why he took on such a daunting task. His reply was, "I have children, grandchildren and great grandchildren that have asked for this story. This is not only my story but their heritage. I only wish I had something like this from my Father."

Barbara Ellen Novak-Lucia-Aigen
Second daughter and transcriber

Anthony and Ann Wedding

Camp Luzerne, Michigan Entrance

Washing Mess-kits in CCC Camp

Walter, Sophie and Baby Frances

Riviera Nigress Hotel

Bunker

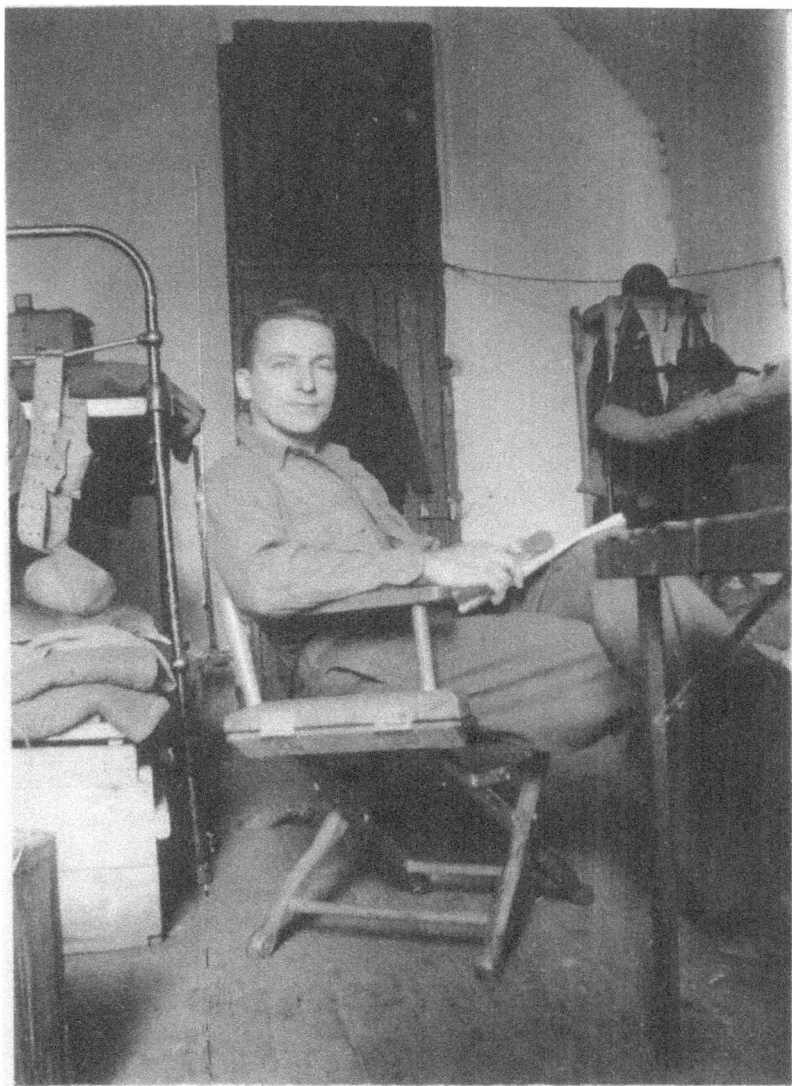

Fort LeHarve

To the Good Life

Walter, relaxed

Walter Novak